Jonathan Ne

Memoirs of a callous picket

Pluto Press

First published in 1983 by Pluto Press Limited
The Works, 105a Torriano Avenue, London NW5 2RX

© Jonathan Neale, 1983

British Library Cataloguing in Publication Data

```
Neale,Jonathan
  Memoirs of a callous picket.
  1.Strikes and lockouts — Hospitals — Great Britain
  I.Title
  331.89'28136211      RA971.35

  ISBN 0-86104-708-7
```

Cover designed by Mikki Rain
Cover photograph by John Sturrock (Network)

Set by Wayside Graphics, Clevedon, Avon
Printed in Great Britain by St Edmundsbury Press
Bury St Edmunds, Suffolk IP33 3TU
Bound by William Brendon Ltd, Tiptree, Essex CO5 0HD

This book is for Steve Ludlam and Myrna Shaw.
Thanks

Contents

Preface / 7

1. **Mop and scalpel** / 9
   Upstairs / 10
   Outside porters / 15
   Downstairs / 17
   Down the road / 19
   Implications / 24

2. **The unions** / 26
   Stewards / 26
   Disciplinary cases / 28
   The steward's job / 31
   Payslips / 35
   The unions / 37
   Union membership / 41
   Shop stewards' committees / 44
   Union leaders / 48
   Whitley councils / 53
   National leaders / 57
   The impact of feminism / 59
   Problems of activists / 64

3. **Struggles** / 66
   Pay policy / 66
   Cuts / 68
   Hospital closures / 70

Staffing levels / 75
Cuts campaigns / 79
Cuts and consciousness / 81
The winter of discontent / 82
Feminism and nurses / 86
Conclusion / 87

4. The battle of 1982 / 89

5. Pray! / 105

Preface

Much of this book is based on personal experience. I have worked in the hospitals as a technician and a porter. I've been a NUPE steward, branch chair and district secretary. The rest of it is based on things hospital workers have told me in various pubs. I've changed the names of the people and the hospitals involved. I've also changed around various details of job and time in order to protect the guilty and avoid giving offence.

A note is in order about 'sexist language'. Through most of the book I have referred to porters and full-time union officials, for instance, as 'he'. I've referred to cleaners and nurses and NALGO stewards as 'she'. I do not mean to imply in any way that there are no male nurses or women porters, or that either sex is better fitted to the job. Mostly, I use 'he' simply because in the specific case I have in mind that particular porter was a man. In other cases, though, I use 'he' or 'she' more generally. I do this because I think it's important that full-time officials are almost always men and cleaners' stewards are almost always women. It's important that cleaning is a woman's job: that's why it is so badly paid. It's important that the unions don't usually appoint women as full-timers: it's part and parcel of the gap between full-timers and members. And the fact that most branch secretaries are men and most cleaners' stewards are women has a critical influence on the way they work with one another.

I owe many debts from my time in the hospitals. Firstly, I owe a general debt over the years to my comrades in the Socialist Workers' Party. Their moral support and political understanding kept me going. I hope this book can do something to help in return towards the building of a revolutionary party in the British working class.

I learned a lot about trade unionism and human nature while working in the hospitals. Among my teachers were Derek Abbey, Olga MacKenzie, Alistair Archibold, Gracie Fowler, Steve Gelfer, Maurice Kolander, Ken Lambaird, Bob Ross, John Clarke, Kambiz Boomla, Roger Frost, Ron Singer, Dave Widgery, Ron Poynter, Lindsay Roth, Millie Farquarson, Theresa Sullivan, Janice Holloway, Sue Dorey, Alison Cartmale, Trevor Hailey, Phil McEntee, Candy Unwin, Anne Drinkwell, Tony Ventham, Dave Blane, Mel Bartley, Sally Mitchison, Robin White, Ray Storey, Bill Tizzard, Bill Geddes, Ian Barber, Mary MacNabb, Anne Robertson, Steve Jeffries and John Deason. I'm grateful to all of them. Heaven forbid any of their friends or employers should hold them responsible for some of the wild opinions in the book.

Several people made critical contributions to the book. My father took me out for a beer, sat me down and told me to stop wasting my time trying to earn a living and just sit down and write my heart out. Sally Mitchison spent years listening to me complain about my work and took over a lot of child care to free me to write. Richard Kuper offered me a contract in return for a reckless promise to produce a book. Without Linda I would never have had the courage to write.

1. Mop and scalpel

For years the press has shown us the two faces of hospital workers. One is the insolent and hang-dog face of the greedy porter. He stands on the picket lines in senseless strikes and turns away ambulances full of pregnant women. He's regularly seen on the evening news, inarticulately trying to defend his indefensible actions. When not on strike he sits around all day long playing cards and making jokes about the afflicted. He is a member of NUPE.

The other side of the coin is the bright scrubbed face of the nurse. She looked after your mum when she was stuck in hospital all those miserable months. She's tireless, dedicated and selfless. She doesn't approve of strikes. She understands, of course, that the porters have a case. But she would never take such an extreme and irresponsible step herself. She wears a little starched bonnet and a tight-waisted uniform. She looks sexy, but clean. She's a member of the Royal College of Nursing.

During 1982 the press encountered some difficulty in reporting the hospital strikes. The angels of mercy came down to stand shoulder to shoulder with the callous NUPE stewards. Indeed, some of them appeared to *be* NUPE stewards. In the midst of a battered and demoralised working class the hospital workers captured the imagination and support of millions of workers. How? What happened? Why?

These are the questions this book will set out to answer. In this chapter, I begin by giving a picture of what it is like to work in a hospital. I try to sketch how the various sorts of work are done, how the workers treat one another, and why they feel they need trade unions. I start with the example of St Agatha's, a prestigious teaching hospital. We begin with the nurses and doctors in the operating theatre, and then move on to look at the lives of porters and cleaners in St Agatha's. At the end of the chapter we move down the road to St Theresa's, and look at the working lives of nurses in this low-status geriatric hospital. The intention of these examples isn't to describe every job but to give the reader a feel for what hospital work is like.

Upstairs

We start at the top: the operating theatre in a teaching hospital. From all over the world medical students come here to watch the skilled surgeons at work. The place is a real 'theatre'. Everything is designed for an audience. There is a clear glass dome in the ceiling. The seats above it are not much used these days. A few of the works staff on their lunch break may lurk up there in the shadows and watch the show. But the serious spectators watch large video screens in the theatre itself, which provide magnified pictures of the operation. Around the theatre stands an admiring throng of nurses and medical students. They wait for the arrival of the surgeons on stage.

The surgeons enter with the quiet self-confidence of men who know their job. They bask in a hundred little rituals of status. 'Good morning, Mr Smith', says the theatre sister. A surgeon is never called 'Dr'. His civilian title harks back to differentials that existed three hundred years ago. Then, doctors were men of polite society who never touched a knife. The title 'doctor' spoke of learning and the book-lined study. Barbers were called in to do the simple dirty jobs like chopping off legs and sewing up wounds. The doctor called the barber 'Mr Smith'. Today, the skilled surgeon considers himself a cut above the family doctor. He clings to the old distinction while reversing the snobbery.

Mr Smith wears jaunty red rubber boots into the theatre. This particular Mr Smith is an eye surgeon who peers through great microscopes as he works. But his colourful boots with the non-slip soles are made for the surgeon who finds himself slipping and sliding in the blood of a road traffic accident.

Each surgeon has his own pet habits, his rituals and foibles. Some insist on playing Bach over the loudspeakers as they operate. Others listen to rugby games on the radio. There are surgeons who scream every time a nurse rustles her uniform. Others keep up a running barrage of lewd remarks to the nurses. Whatever the ritual, the theatre falls into line. These men are prima donnas. They do difficult and taxing work which requires all their concentration. Their skill matters; not least to the owner of the unconscious body on the table. They're under great pressure and they relieve it as they will. They may be childish or temperamental. But they're in charge. And nobody wants to rattle a surgeon so that his mind wanders and his hand shakes.

The oldest and most distinguished of the surgeons is also the most impossibly childish. A technician will spend fifteen minutes tinkering with a complex piece of machinery while the surgeon nags and insults him. Then he will stay and watch the surgery, transfixed by the gentle knowing fingers at work. He wanders out into the corridor and says to another technician, 'That man, he's a real swine. But oh, the beauty of what he does.'

The nurses are the main audience for the doctors. Three or four nurses attend each case. They prepare the instrument tray for each operation and hand the surgeon the tools as he asks for them. It's their job to know in advance which instruments each surgeon favours for a particular operation. If they get it wrong the youngest nurse has to run breathlessly for the right instrument. It's also their job to stand and watch and to clean up afterwards.

Doctors and nurses have a curious relationship here. At first it seems coolly professional. The nurses do a useful job as part of a team. They do it well, and they're proud of their work. Yet there are echoes of the doctor–nurse books, too.

The majority of nurses are women. Many things about the job recall woman's traditional place in the family. 'Nurse' is itself the word for giving breast milk to a baby. By extension, it is used for the whole business of caring for small children and other helpless people. The senior nurse in charge of a ward is called 'sister'. The nurse in charge of a whole hospital is called 'matron'.

Of course, not all nurses are women. For instance, one of the operating theatres has a man in charge. His official title is 'nursing officer'. He prefers to be called 'sister'. The word stands for what he's achieved. Many nurses are men. But nursing is none the less thought of as a woman's job because caring for the helpless is women's work.

If the nurse is mother to the patient and daughter to the boss, she is mistress and secretary to the doctor. Her very attitude of admiring service in the theatre recalls many women's roles. So does the way she runs for what the doctor wants. The theatre itself is filled with sexual innuendo and harmless flirting. Doctors and workers all wear the same thin and comfortable uniforms. On the wards, sexuality is more restrained. It's insensitive to flaunt your bodily health in front of the sick and their relatives. More important, though, this restraint is linked to a long tradition of nursing that stretches back to Florence Nightingale. This tradition centres on cleanliness. The key word is 'sterile'. On one level, it's a reaction to the mud and filth of the Crimean War and the constant infections of the nineteenth-century hospital.

But there's more to it. The emphasis is no longer on keeping just the patients clean. Nowadays, the cleaners clean the wards and the laundry cleans the clothes. The idea is to keep *the nurse* clean. Before Nightingale, nurses were low and dirty women. Any woman who works with her hands covered in urine and faeces and blood and pus is in danger of being seen as slightly low class – especially if it's also her job to wash men's bottoms and genitals. But by 1900 the nursing profession had made it clear that nothing of the kind was true. They scrubbed and scrubbed and scrubbed.

There was another reason for seeing nurses as low women. They were working women who lived away from home in great dormitories. They had control of their own money. It was inevitable that there would be suspicions of sexual activity. So matron was supposed to watch over her charges carefully to preserve the reputation of the profession. Of course, they haven't been able to prevent nurses behaving like everybody else. But management has made sure that nurses aren't flagrant: their sexuality is controlled.

That's what the uniforms are all about. Nurses have to wear silly bonnets, like milkmaids. They have starched aprons, like country-house servants in the 1930s. Those aprons are important.

If they aren't properly starched or tied the nurse responsible can be called into matron's office and given a dressing down. During the 1982 pay campaign one group of nurses was nervous about what they wore on the picket line. They thought they would be disciplined for wearing their uniforms outside the hospital. In the event, management took the nursing steward aside and asked her to ensure that all nurses had proper aprons on at all times on the picket line.

The uniforms are close fitting. They have broad belts which accentuate the breasts above and the hips below. But decoration is right out. The nurse who wears coloured tights to work will find herself sent straight home. Many nursing schools forbid earrings. Some even forbid the little gold studs necessary to keep newly pierced ears open and uninfected. Unions have been built among nurses over coloured tights and earrings.

The point is that the nurse's sexuality should be emphasised, but not owned up to. She can *look* sexually attractive, but she can't *be* sexual. A nurse is set up as an embodiment of all that is best in women. And she is therefore *passive*.

Of course, nurses are real women and real women are not like that. Many nurses are real men. But in this operating theatre the cast is mostly made up of active confident upper-class men and quiet admiring middle-class women. It's a play often seen on television, and it has seduced many girls into nursing.

The theatre hierarchy is not only sexual. Race and class play their part. The surgeons are almost all white men. The anaesthetists are the doctors who administer the drugs and watch throughout the operation to make sure the patient doesn't turn blue. They are not thought to be as skilled as surgeons. Some of them are white women and some are Asian men. The consultant anaesthetist is a white man.

One technician helps each anaesthetist. Half the technicians are immigrants and half are English. All are skilled working men and proud of it. The one black technician flirts a lot with one of the white sisters. It helps them both to pass the time. Nursing management has spoken to her about this several times. She pays no attention. She isn't doing anything with him outside the theatre, and she isn't going to be told what to do.

Many nurses marry manual workers. But this is an elite hospital. Nursing management will speak to the nurse who consorts with a porter. Doctors are felt to be more appropriate. A few of the sisters have in fact married immigrant doctors.

Below the technicians in this operating theatre are three porters and a lone cleaner. They are white and unskilled. She is black. Inside the theatre they are almost invisible.

The theatre's a hierarchical world. It's also jealous and competitive. But every once in a while the workers suddenly pull together in an emergency. The technician notices that the patient's toes are going blue. He moves quickly to whisper in the anaesthetist's ear. She looks the patient over rapidly and says to the surgeons, 'I'm sorry, the patient is having a cardiac arrest.' Everybody moves like lightning in the eerie quiet. The surgeons keep their heads down and sew up the operation wound. A technician and a porter run down the corridor for the cardiac arrest machine. The head technician climbs on the table and begins to pound the chest. As he tires, sister takes over. The machine arrives. The anaesthetist puts its greased electric pads on either side of the heart. He nods at the nurse standing by the switch and she turns it on. The patient's heart jumps and the machine's screen suddenly shows a normal pattern. The nurse unhooks the machine. The surgeon announces they have tied everything up. A porter has already called an ambulance crew to take the patient to intensive care. The two other porters load the patient onto a trolley as the anaesthetist hovers. The nurse cleans up. An hour later news arrives that the patient has woken up in intensive care and asked crossly for a cup of tea.

Like a well-drilled army, everybody has done the right thing at the right time, with no orders given. Each works as a member of a team, and each trusts the others. They are united by their various skills and the importance of the work they do.

This is part of what makes hospital workers different from factory workers. The theatre has a more rigid hierarchy than any factory. But the hierarchy seems more justifiable to the workers. The surgeon isn't just using class power when he behaves like a pig to the technician. He's also nervous. The team isn't just a pyramid of privilege, it's a group of dedicated people, too. The nurses aren't spectators in their own lives. They're part of a great drama.

'Scalpel please, nurse.'

Outside porters

The theatre is all glamour. Beyond its shining glass doors sit the outside porters. They're not glamorous. They're bored. Their job is to bring terrified patients down from the ward on trolleys and return groggy ones upstairs. There are two pairs of porters on duty each day. One pair works from 8 a.m. to 5 p.m., and the other from 10 a.m. till the last case of the day. For most of the day, at least one pair is sitting on the bench in the corridor outside the theatre. They are waiting for the order to fetch a patient. They study the form, do the crosswords, read every word in the *Sun* and the *Mirror* four times, argue about last night's TV, and complain about how bored they are. There's nothing to do, but they can't go and pass the time somewhere else. The surgeons are never sure how long any operation will last. Operating-theatre time is like gold dust and surgeons try to cram as many patients as possible into one session. So for the outside porters, long stretches of nothing alternate with mad rushes where everybody screams at them to get the patient down.

Insults aggravate the boredom. All day long, busy nurses and surgeons pass up and down the theatre corridor. The porters greet them as they go by. Many walk by without returning the greeting. Many make some crack like 'I wish I had your job, sitting there doing nothing.' It's humiliating, but the porters daren't talk back. They would be down in the office next day if they did. They're trapped. They have to sit there looking lazy. It's their job.

The outside porters want the union to get two things from management. First, they want a little room off the corridor for themselves. Then they won't have to sit in public doing nothing. Second, they want regrading from grade three to grade four. It isn't the money that matters. That's only sixty pence a week before tax. It's that the inside porters are grade four, and look down on them.

There are three inside porters at this hospital. Their job is to push the patients in and out of each of the four operating theatres and lift them on and off the operating table. They, too, spend a lot of their time waiting around. There is no more skill to their job. But some of the glamour of the theatre rubs off on them.

They stay inside, and the outside porters stay outside. Between them is a 'sterile barrier'. To enter the theatre you must wash and then put on special clothes and hat and mask and shoes. To leave, you change back into mufti. It takes five minutes each way. So the inside porters stay inside for their tea breaks. They get free tea and biscuits with the technicians and male nurses. They dress in the same clothes as the surgeons. When the outside porters bring a patient down, they stop at the theatre entrance. The inside porters slide the patient onto a clean trolley inside the theatre and wheel it in. As they do so, they sometimes make remarks about the awkward way the outside porters handle transfers. The inside porters relay to the outside porters the instructions to bring patients down. They pass on the instructions to hurry up and the nagging when the outside porters get behind. The necessary sterile barrier becomes a social barricade.

That's why the outside porters mind about being grade three. They're not saying that the inside porters shouldn't be grade four. But they know they're as good as the inside men.

Hospitals are rife with small disputes over grading. The system of grading is complex beyond belief. There are seventeen grades of ancillary worker. They include catering staff, porters, domestics and laundry workers. Grade six, for instance, covers butchers, sterile supply chargehands, laundry machine chargehands, hairdressers, head herdsmen, operating theatre attendants, trainee operating department assistants, propagating gardeners, senior shoe-makers, steam stokers, tailors in charge, bakers, cooks and domestic supervisors. It also includes some sorts of blood transfusion drivers, shop managers and storekeepers, but not other sorts.

Porters are found on grades two, three and four. Chargehand porters are five. Assistant cooks are four, cooks are six and senior cooks are eight. The grading system sets out the relative value of everybody's labour to the nearest halfpence per hour. More skill will gain you a couple of grades. So will being a supervisor. A man's job is usually two or three grades higher than a comparable job done by a woman. The sums of money marking the differentials are trivial. The judgements are important.

Let no one think that this elaborate hierarchy was invented by ancillaries. There are eighteen pay scales for nursing staff, most of them with six different incremental points. There are forty-one pay scales for administrative and clerical staff (forty-three if you include scales 16A and 19A). Each of these scales has five to seven incremental points. There are separate uniforms for medical students, doctors, technicians, cleaners, ward orderlies, domestic supervisors, ward clerks, pupil nurses, trainee nurses, auxiliary nurses, enrolled nurses, agency nurses, staff nurses, sisters, nurse tutors, male nurses, works staff, porters, trainee occupational therapists, occupational therapists, occupational therapy aides, trainee physiotherapists, physiotherapists, physiotherapy aides, and so on. Most hospital workers can tell at a glance who they're dealing with, though in a big hospital it can take a year to sort out some of the more specialist uniforms. It's a complex world where everyone has a defined place in the pecking order. Most hospital workers react by feeling they should be at least one point up in the hierarchy.

The outside porters sit barred from the clubland world of beautiful surgery and obliging women beyond the glass doors. They feel worthless. If you ask them what they do, they sometimes say, 'I'm just a porter.' But they demand that management give them that extra point and recognise their equal worth.

Downstairs

There was one cleaner in the operating theatre. She was socially invisible. Most other cleaners in the hospital were too. Each worked in a ward or a department on her own. The cleaners wanted two things from the union. They wanted something done about the contractors, and they wanted something done about their rest room in the basement.

The contractors were the immediate problem. The hospital had sub-contracted the cleaning to a private firm. It was agreed that the firm would continue to pay NHS wages and get as much work done as before. But the contractors also had to pay their supervisors and make a profit. So they had to get more done with fewer workers. The cleaners had already been working quite hard. The solution was to drive them harder and to turn a blind eye if they skimped part of the job. Usually, the bit they skimped was noticed by the ward sister or the head of department. The sister or head would then nag the cleaner. The cleaner was caught in the middle. She worked as hard as she could, but never really caught up. The cleaners wanted something done about the un-ending strain.

The other thing the cleaners wanted was a new rest room. They had two breaks a day: half-an-hour in the morning and half-an-hour for lunch. They all took their breaks in one rest room in the basement. They couldn't afford to eat in the canteen. They weren't comfortable on the wards. They were black and Spanish working-class women. The black cleaners liked to laugh and shout in their breaks. The Spaniards liked to argue twenty to the dozen. The atmosphere on the wards was not for them. They couldn't behave like they did at home. Like the outside porters and like all of us, they needed their own lair: their rest room.

It was a slum. There was no water and no cooker. There wasn't even an electric kettle. There were no windows because it was deep inside the basement. There weren't enough chairs to go round. So some people sat on other people's laps to eat their lunch. The lockers were old and cranky and unsafe for keeping personal belongings. The walls were unpainted, the lino tatty, the carpets worse. And because there was no water, there were no sinks and no mirrors.

That's what really hurt. The rest room was where they changed before starting work. It was where they changed back again before going home to husband or lover. They wanted to see their faces to check their make-up and their hair. But management hadn't put in any 'vanity sets' because it didn't matter if they were beautiful.

It mattered for other people. Everybody else had a nicer rest room. The deputy manager was a woman. She had her own personal toilet. Every time she ran out of toilet paper she got on the phone to tell the head porter the change the roll – urgently. Right next to the cleaners' room was the changing room for women doctors and clerical staff. It was lovely. There were tiled vanity units, modern lockers, and lighting that didn't look like cop shop surplus. It had been redone the year before. If they could have it, why couldn't the cleaners? Even the porters had windows and an electric kettle in their basement hole.

The answer was easy. The cleaners were on the bottom. They were grade one ancillaries, because cleaning is the easiest and least skilled work there is. After all, any woman can do it. They were immigrants. All that immigrant cleaners need are the facilities that will do for Mrs Mop. That's why the cleaners cared so much about the rest room. It stood for the rest of their lives.

Down the road

St Agatha's Hospital is a prestigious specialist hospital. Down the road, there's St Theresa's Hospital; it represents the other end of the National Health Service. Its architecture proclaims it was once the local workhouse. One patient remembers those days. She's lived round the corner all her life. 'Now,' she says, 'they call it a hospital.' She smiles.

She's got a point. St Theresa's is a hospital for working-class geriatric cases. Most patients aren't acutely ill. They're just worn out and alone. Many of them are widows whose children moved out of the area after the war. Gradually, it becomes obvious to their neighbours or doctors or children that they simply can't cope on their own. The council makes little provision for old people's homes. So they come into hospital under one diagnosis or another. They stay because there is nowhere else for them to go.

Doctors and nurses avoid places like St Theresa's. Nearby, there are hospitals which provide high technology medicine to acute and interesting cases. At St Theresa's the cases are medically boring. There's often little the doctor can do. Geriatric medicine carries low status in the medical world: somewhere below venereology. And that low status is reflected in the composition of the workforce.

The consultants are the only white male doctors. The house officers are Asians and English women. Many are marking time until they can get a better job.

Management also has problems hiring nursing staff. It's difficult to attract state registered nurses to a geriatric hospital. Most of the ward staff are state enrolled nurses and nursing auxiliaries. Enrolled nurses are a special British institution. They're recognised nowhere else in the world. They do two years' training instead of three. The emphasis is on practical matters rather than book learning. Entrance requirements are lower. So are wages. A registered nurse can be promoted to sister and beyond. An enrolled nurse can never be promoted.

The enrolled grade stems from an old compromise. The administrators of the old workhouses and Poor Law hospitals needed more nurses and couldn't get them. The nursing hierarchy didn't want unqualified and unprofessional people. So the enrolled grade was introduced: professional nurses, destined for the bottom jobs.

St Theresa's can't attract nearly enough enrolled nurses either. Much of the work is done by untrained auxiliary nurses. They're hired off the street and thrown onto the job. On her first day, one auxiliary was left alone on the ward to give tea to twenty patients. She dithered around without any idea of what to do. One of the patients' relatives came up to her. 'It's alright, dear, I've been visiting dad for years. I'll show you how.' That's how she learned the job.

The sisters at St Theresa's are all registered nurses. They look on the enrolled nurses as nice girls, but not too bright. The enrolled nurses look down on the auxiliaries in their turn.

'You don't know what it's like here. They hear you're an auxiliary, they figure you got nothing between your ears.' There are constant remarks. Little reminders about not handing out the drugs. Comments about how some people can write notes and others can't. Other times, it's convenient for the auxiliary to be 'responsible'. On the night shift, the enrolled nurse often goes off and leaves the auxiliary to mind the ward for three hours on her own.

The auxiliaries resent the way they're treated. They can see that nursing is about *caring*: washing, moving, changing, talking and cuddling. For this you don't have to be a 'professional'. It calls for a human being. The auxiliaries feel they can do that as well as the qualified staff.

You might expect the standard of nurses hired here to be very low. Actually, it isn't. There are two reasons. The first is racism. Quiet racism is rife in nursing. In true British fashion, nothing is said about it openly. But it's black nurses and auxiliaries who fill most of the posts at St Theresa's. There are black faces at St Agatha's, too, but they stand out there. Here, they're the norm. The competent black nurse who finds herself stuck at St Theresa's has reason to feel bitter. The patients have reason to feel grateful.

The second reason is the enrolled nurses and auxiliaries. They may not have a lot of A-levels. But somebody who works hard and cares is more use than somebody who's academically qualified and doesn't. That said, the nursing care is pretty basic because of chronic understaffing. This is not an area of medicine to which the best resources are directed.

On one male ward, two nurses come on at 7.30 a.m. There should really be five on this ward. They give out breakfasts. They take the patients to the toilet. They wash patients by putting them in a hoist and dipping them in the bath. They dress them, give them lunch, and toilet them again. Then they wash the patients they haven't done yet. It can be two in the afternoon by the time the last patient is out of bed. Almost time for tea, and toilet, and starting them back to bed, and dinner and toilet. You miss your dinner, your back aches, there's hardly time to sit down. Your day off you spend sleeping. When you've finished the basics of washing and dressing and food: that's it. You sit down for the break you should have had two hours ago.

The result is that patients don't get what they need. The nurses start to hate the patients or just switch off inside. Again and again, you find yourself alone on the ward trying to dress a recalcitrant patient. Just as you've almost got his trousers on, three men scream for urine bottles. Old Mr Higgins gets up to walk across the room without his frame. If you don't get to him fast, he's going to take another fall – or, worse still, escape off the ward. Then sister from the next ward will bring him back and ask what you think you're doing. You know you can only get to one of those men with a bottle in time, and the other two will wet themselves. Then you'll have to clean them later. And they'll be one step nearer to 'habitual incontinence'. They know that, too, which is why they're screaming at you. And Mr Higgins snarls at you when you put an arm out to stop him getting away. He's not wandering. He's trying to get out of the hospital. He hates it here.

The first time all this happens, you're appalled and burst into tears; the hundredth time, you harden your heart. You pretend the patients aren't people. Later, you find yourself screaming at Mr Higgins and the men who want bottles and the man you're changing. After three years, a bullying undertone permanently cuts through your voice.

That's if you last three years. Usually, you don't. Auxiliaries come and go like people through a revolving door. Enrolled nurses get out as fast as they can. Body and heart wear out. Sickness rates are high. The more sickness and turnover there is, the more new staff you have. You have to show them how to do everything. It's unlikely that management will hire a temp from the agency to replace a sick nurse. The more you work short-staffed, the harder you work – and the more likely you are to go sick or quit yourself.

It's difficult to work in a geriatric hospital. It's harder to live there. Many patients are lonely. They're usually widows, and they are often cut off from their children. They suffer from multiple ailments, many of them relentlessly painful. Harbingers of senility and decay surround them. It takes great courage and largeness of heart to be a geriatric patient. Most young people don't have those qualities. Geriatric patients need all the admiration and emotional support they can get.

Instead, they get a thousand little cuts. First, the nurse can't get Jim to the toilet in his wheelchair every time he needs to go. He seems to have to urinate every hour. He's a big man to lift. She daren't leave the ward for long. She's got too much to do. So

Jim gets used to using a urine bottle. Soon he doesn't mind if sometimes there's no curtain to hide behind while he uses it. Then there comes the day when the nurse can't get to him until five minutes after he yells for a bottle. He wets himself. He's humiliated, and apologises to the nurse all day. She reassures him that it doesn't matter. They're being kind, but it *does* matter. Or did, to the kind of man Jim used to be.

Then there's the boredom and the resentment. You're stuck in bed till noon because there aren't enough people to change you. After that, you're parked in rows in front of the television. It's cartoons if you're lucky and the Labour Party Conference if you're not. In the evening, you miss the international football on television, because the day staff have to get everybody in bed before the night staff come on.

It seems like you never get out of your chair. You need the physiotherapist's help to walk – and the most you'll get is a few minutes a day. You wait three days before the nurses shave your beard. You stop caring about your appearance. Anyway, the hospital seems to dress you in jumble-sale clothes. You get different ones back from the laundry each time. The collars are frayed. Your arthritic hands spend half-an-hour tugging at a stuck zipper. You want to get it done up before your wife comes by with the grandchildren and they see granddad a drooling mess. The man in the next bed is senile and angry. He keeps calling the nurses 'fucking cunts'. You hope he doesn't do it while the kids are here. You hope you aren't going to get like him. You fear you will.

Nobody talks to you.

The ward is the scene of many little human tragedies. As a nurse, you survive by blanking out. In the process, you become a worse nurse. You blank out your feelings and the patients' feelings. You start treating them as objects or children or 'patients'. Anything but adults coping with difficult problems. You treat the room as your ward, not their home. You avoid talking to them.

What's worse, you know you're doing it. You still hate the job. You still see the misery. You see how little you can do about it. You sense, resentfully, that something good inside you is being strangled. And you know what that 'something good' is. It's what brought you into nursing to start with. It's your feeling for people, your wish to be of help, to comfort, to mother, to nurse. Of course, you also thought there'd be a little glamour with the job. What about it? The image of the starched nurse in the operating theatre? The pride in telling people in the pub you were a nurse? The education and the professionalism? That, too, is mocked by your working life.

You came to this work out of love and pride. You find yourself up to the elbows in some ungrateful old man's shit.

Implications

We've seen something of the working lives of theatre nurses, porters, cleaners and ward nurses. There are many more kinds of hospital workers: telephonists and radiographers, clerks and canteen staff, electricians and laundry workers. There are many kinds of hospital. St Agatha's is different from St Theresa's. A district general hospital is different from both, and a district mental hospital different from all of them. Each job in each hospital is special. But it's still possible to make some general observations about hospital work and hospital politics.

First of all, notice what a hierarchical world it is. Everybody is obsessed with their place in the pecking order. The outside porters worry about their grading, the theatre nurses are proud of working in a teaching hospital and rude to the porters, the geriatric nurses observe fine distinctions among themselves. This hierarchy is validated by the skill of the people at the top: the doctors. Building workers treat their site agent with barely veiled contempt. Hospital workers echo the technician on the surgeon: a swine – but the beauty of what he does.

Hospital consciousness is very sectional. Nurses stick with nurses, cooks with cooks. There are countless petty jealousies. Resentments and snobberies divide the workforce. Many hospital workers feel they're not really workers at all. Rather they're some sort of dwarf doctor. 'Professional' and 'para-medical' are the words used.

In all of this, the manual workers are rather pushed to one

side. In local government, cleaners and cooks are called 'manual workers'. In hospitals they're called ancillaries. The word makes them sound like some sort of optional extra, a frill on the real workforce. But when the ancillaries go on strike, everybody starts to scream about how necessary they are to the patients. It's often only then that the ancillaries themselves realise how central they are.

In a factory or shipyard, the manual workers are socially dominant. In hospitals they are only about half the workforce. And a defensive half at that. Like the cleaners with their rest room, they don't feel the hospital is a working-class place. At the same time, the hospital keeps rubbing their noses in their low status. This produces defensive pride, like the outside porters who wanted their own place to retreat to.

Notice also how the family system and racism pattern and reinforce the hierarchy. This is obvious with nurses. But notice also that men carry things and fix things; women clean things and care for people. Racism makes black women into cleaners. It also makes Asian graduates into anaesthetists.

All this makes for a divided and confused workforce. The pattern of class consciousness differs from that of a Bolshevik munitions factory. Nevertheless, most of these people are, and see themselves as workers. Although the theatre nurses don't belong to unions at St Agatha's, at other hospitals they do. The theatre technicians described in this chapter belong to unions. So do the porters, the cleaners and the ward nurses. There is no closed shop. They belong to unions because they know they're workers and think a union card's a good idea. In the next chapter we will look at how their unions work.

2. The unions

Stewards

This chapter describes the day-to-day workings of hospital unions. The central figure in these unions is the ancillary workers' steward. So we'll begin with her.

Senior union people are always on the lookout for likely stewards. Anybody who seems articulate, or even just plain angry, will usually be encouraged to become a steward. There's rarely a contested election. It isn't that the unions are undemocratic. It's just rare for two workers in one section to be willing to become stewards. And if there are two willing and able people, the other stewards encourage both to become stewards, so they can support each other.

The usual pattern is that the branch secretary or senior steward simply bestows the office of shop steward. Often it's necessary to hold a meeting. Partly this is to legitimate their position as steward. But mostly it's a way to force them to take on the job. Take Shirley. For days before the meeting, the branch secretary keeps telling her that she'll make a good steward. Then at the meeting he says that the canteen really needs a steward. He thinks Shirley would make a good one. All her friends in the canteen turn to look at her and shout happily that she should do it. Her hands fly up to cover her face. The branch secretary asks if she'll do it. In a small voice she agrees. Everybody laughs happily.

This is the common pattern because most people don't want to become stewards. They have good reason. A good active steward is marked down by management. The frighteners are on. Tom, the porters' steward, is constantly watched. Before, it was OK to sneak out to the pub for a quick pint. Now that he's steward he'll lose his job if anybody reports him. On the late shift he used to go home when the job was finished and somebody would clock him out. Now, he stays to the end of the shift twiddling his thumbs.

When you're a steward you never lose this feeling of being watched. And it ruins your relationship with your immediate boss. Shirley's bosses are constantly hassling her to give Shirley a rough time. If she refuses, Shirley feels bad because someone's having a bad time on her account. Usually, the boss does give her a bad time. There are unending niggling questions. Why haven't you finished that little job? Why were you five minutes late back from tea? Do you really need to take your holiday that week just because that's when your husband has his holiday?

Sometimes the steward is put on unpleasant or meaningless jobs. Portering stewards can find themselves going down to the mortuary a lot. One creative management in London put a white-collar steward in a little office on her own. She had a grandiose job title and nothing whatsoever to do. Nine months later she had a nervous breakdown.

Being a steward can also create a lot of tension with your fellow-workers. For example, let's say there are two women in the laundry to do the folding and packing. One of them is elected steward. Every time the steward does something for the union the other woman covers for her. The other woman is usually understanding. Still, there are limits to anybody's understanding when it means doing somebody else's work. The more boring and unpleasant the work, the more tension there is. The steward is understandably happy to get away from the boring grind of work. She particularly likes long meetings with other stewards. She's not at work, she's talking to pleasant and interesting people, and she doesn't have to deal with those toads from management. But she can't go to too many meetings. Her fellow-worker feels that these meetings can't all be really necessary. Sometimes she says so. The steward usually sees her point. The steward also knows that any representative who alienates her own members is wide open to victimisation.

Many people don't want to be stewards simply because they feel that they couldn't do the job well. This isn't surprising. Most hospital ancillaries are 'unskilled' women. Their lives have been one long lesson in what they can't do in the world. They feel particularly inadequate in the middle-class world of management, negotiations and letters. Often, only one person in a union branch feels comfortable writing an official letter, and that person writes them all. Indeed, one of the reasons why the branch *secretary* has traditionally been the key person in many unions is that *writing* well is such a rare skill. For many, just sitting down in the office and talking management's language is scary.

Of course, some people do want to become stewards. But even they feign reluctance. British manual workers frown on public displays of ambition, and nobody trusts ambition in a politician.

So when Shirley hides her face in her hands, it's not beyond possibility that she's a militant socialist who's been plotting for a year to get herself elected.

Disciplinary cases

In any case, Shirley's mates are happy to nominate her. They know they need a good steward in case they get into trouble. And there are many ways a hospital worker can land up in trouble. For one thing, they have too many bosses. A porter is supposed to be responsible to the head porter. But if the pharmacist feels he's late taking the drugs to the ward, he complains. So the porter does the pharmacy first and X-ray is on the phone about how he hasn't brought down their patients. Sister from Churchill Ward hears him swearing about X-ray in the lift and reports him for using bad language.

Hospitals are very decorous places, and manual workers are constantly under the eye of white-collar supervisors. Remarks which are the commonplace of human interaction on a building site can mean instant dismissal in a hospital. A personal row over who does the washing up on the ward can end with both orderly and cleaner down in the office. And it's in the nature of hospital work that an awful lot of simple mistakes can spell danger for the patient. A nurse who is left by herself on the ward may try to lift a patient; that patient may well end up on the floor. One big reason nurses join unions is that every time this happens they are in trouble – but nobody ever asks why they were left alone to start with.

The most common cause of disciplinary cases, though, is the tension between supervisor and worker. Lateness or answering back or swearing or taking an extra five minutes at lunch don't automatically lead to a disciplinary hearing. The supervisor has considerable discretion. It's usually the supervisor's choice to report somebody. Some heads of department generate far more than their share of disciplinaries. This means that workers see their own disciplinary troubles as the result of arbitrary malevolence by the supervisor. If the head porter has a quiet word when one of his blokes is an hour late, why should the chief engineer have me up in the office for being fifteen minutes late?

The answer is usually that there is a struggle for power in the section. Sometimes this is because the supervisor is a bossy person, but has no personality to back it up. So the threat of higher management is used. Sometimes it's because the supervisor is under pressure from above to produce more work. Sometimes it's because the workers are organising and asserting themselves.

An example of one small works department will illustrate all these processes. The chief engineer in this department arrived on the job straight from engineering college with hardly a clue about how all the machines in the basement actually worked. He sensibly relied on the engineers in boiler suits to explain it to him. They became friendly and shared many cups of coffee.

The shift engineers also started to do a lot of overtime. They were responsible for the boilers and emergency maintenance throughout the hospital. They worked a rotary shift: earlies one week, lates the next, and then nights for a week. When there was a work overload, the shifts overlapped and they worked in pairs. The chief engineer couldn't tell how many men the job needed, so they took as much overtime as they needed. Eventually, the finance department came down on the chief engineer. Enraged, he set out to whip the men into line.

One lunchtime, one of the men got drunk in the pub and stormed up to the chief engineer's office to have a go about overtime. 'If you don't like it, resign,' said the chief. 'I bloody well will,' came the reply. The chief told his secretary to type out a resignation immediately. The angry shift engineer signed it and went home.

Next morning he woke up with a hangover and realised what he'd done. He wanted his job back. The chief had him by the book, but the men didn't think it was fair. They went on strike for a week. The chief engineer and two other men scabbed all week and the strike folded. From then on it was war. Bosses and workers insulted each other whenever nobody was watching.

One of the men, Harry, was particularly vulnerable. Everybody knew he saved a couple of months' rent from time to time by living in various corners of the hospital. He was a single man on crazy shifts, and he didn't mind. One day the chief engineer was pretty sure he'd finally caught the man. In the electrical plant room on the roof he found underwear, a shirt, trousers, a comb and bedding. He called in the union and pointed out that this was against the rules. The steward realised they had no proof of identity, or they would have produced it. He denied that those were Harry's clothes and asked for evidence. The steward admitted that the clothes were a small size and Harry was a small man. But Harry, he said, had a sense of style. He'd never be caught dead in clothes like that. Look at the cut of the trousers, for God's sake. Flares! Flares went out two years ago. Not Harry's. No way.

They couldn't prove it and Harry got off. But the chief engineer kept after him. One night the chief came in at two in the morning on Harry's shift. The basement lights were turned off and the boiler room was in darkness. He found Harry sitting in a chair in the boiler room. He had his feet up on another chair and his shoes and socks off. The jubilant chief suspended Harry on the spot. He sent the man home and finished the shift himself.

Next day, Harry and his steward went down to the personnel office, with the chief engineer. The chief engineer outlined the case to the personnel woman, a young sociology graduate. The steward couldn't see any way out of this one. Sleeping on the job is a summary dismissal offence. The personnel woman asked Harry if the chief engineer's account was correct.

'Yes.'

'Then I'm afraid I have no alternative but to dismiss you. Sleeping on the job is an offence warranting summary dismissal, especially in a responsible position such as you hold.'

'I wasn't sleeping,' Harry said.

'Then how do you explain the circumstances?'

Everybody looked at Harry. The steward felt sick. He was losing his friends in the works department one by one as the chief engineer drove them out. He didn't see what Harry could say.

'I was masturbating,' Harry said.

Nothing in the book mentioned that as a summary offence. Wrong, of course. But if you waited until two in the morning and took the precaution of turning off all the lights, you were hardly doing it in public. Harry still had his paging bleep with him. So anybody who needed a shift engineer in a hurry could have raised him in the normal way.

Such was the steward's suddenly inspired argument. Management didn't really buy it. Nor did they fancy arguing the matter at an industrial tribunal. They compromised on a final warning.

The steward's job

Disciplinaries, then, usually grow out of tension between worker and supervisor. The supervisor uses management's authority. Going down to the office is a lot like going down to the head teacher's office when you were a child. They tell you a few hours ahead of time and let you sweat it out. Often you spend the time trying to guess what it's about. When you get down there you hang around for a few minutes until the right time. Then you knock gently on the door. He* calls you in. He wears a suit and speaks in carefully modulated tones. He calls you 'Mr Gonzalez', with formal politeness. He's on the other side of a large desk in what seems to be an enormous room. You want a cigarette but suspect it would be cheeky to light one. Anyway, the only ashtray is across the room on his desk and you'd have to get up to use it. Your foreman is sitting in a corner of the room. When you look at

*In this particular case, all participants were male. I've chosen to keep to gender vocabulary for reasons explained fully in the preface.

management, you can't see the foreman. When you turn to talk to the foreman, you're conscious of management's eyes looking at the side of your head. They outnumber you, and management treats you like a child. 'What do you have to say to that, Mr Gonzales?' 'Didn't you think before you . . .' 'We all have to observe certain rules, you know.' 'I don't want you to think I'm being unreasonable, but if everybody . . .' 'I'm afraid I have to take a very serious view of this matter.'

Actually, he's not afraid. You are. You learned the fear in school. Every day of your working life has reinforced the fear. And you're also angry at the injustice of it all. That bastard didn't need to drag you down here. If only you could make management understand what is really going on down there in the mess room. But you're afraid that when you open your mouth so much anger will spill out that you'll lose your job for sure. Your defence is incoherent. After the final lecture you walk out of the office, feeling hard done by. And also you feel a fool. Next time you're called to the office, you take a steward with you.

But the steward herself is usually in a weak position in defending a disciplinary case. The power of unions comes from what workers are prepared to do together. Every steward knows she is only as strong as her members make her. And she knows that in defending an individual case she usually has little to fall back on. If Anne's in trouble, her fellow-workers may well feel it's unfair. But that doesn't necessarily mean they're prepared to do anything about it. Sometimes they don't even like Anne. Many supervisors have an instinct for attacking the weak.

It isn't just that each disciplinary hearing deals with an individual case. It's also that individual cases are the steward's main job. Wages and fringe benefits are negotiated nationally. It's wages that unite workers. It's individual cases that divide them. The hospital steward is in a far weaker position than the factory steward who negotiates piecework and annual rises.

Moreover, the steward knows she'll be back in the same office again tomorrow. If she alienates management today, somebody else will pay. She can rub management's face in it when she has a stupid supervisor who's overstepped the mark. But then they're not going to listen tomorrow to her pleas to turn a summary dismissal into a final warning. The steward doesn't have to like individual members of management. But she has to have a working relationship with them.

The steward holds a few cards and has to argue the case in management's terms. 'By the book', it's called. Management wrote most of the book. And arguing by the book ignores what's really happening. That runs much deeper than the alleged offence. Take the example of a cleaner called Maria. The sister on her ward took pride in a squeaky clean ward. The domestic supervisor kept taking her off to do bits of other wards. Maria was caught between them.

Maria had been a beauty in her youth. At forty, she was a greying but still handsome woman. But her body was beginning to betray her under the pressure of work. Her back hurt constantly. She'd been off with it for a few months, but didn't dare take more time away. The pain made her crabby. It ate away at the edges of her married life. She could feel herself developing an old woman's lines and querulous voice.

The pain was worst when she bent over and pushed. Cleaning floors involved a lot of that. Particularly hard was vacuuming the small carpeted section in the corner of the ward. The vacuum cleaner they gave her was too short and she had to bend extra far. Really, she shouldn't have been cleaning floors at all. But she had to live. So lots of days she left the small carpeted section till the last, and then the supervisor came and took her off to do another job. Each time this happened, sister was down on her like a ton of bricks. Day in, day out they sniped at each other about that bit of floor. One day, something in Maria snapped. She exploded at sister in Spanish. Sister understood little of the torrent except for the English phrases 'bloody bastard' and 'fucking bitch'. Sister had subscribed to the *Daily Worker* in her youth and didn't like getting people in trouble. But she'd also been raised a good Irish Catholic and there were things nobody said to her. She was down to the office like a shot.

The next day, the stewards were down there with Maria. The issue was no longer Maria's work, her body, or her life. The issue was that she had sworn at sister. The stewards and Maria cobbled together a hasty defence outside the office door – in English.

Then they went into the office and said Maria spoke no English. Everybody waited while the personnel officer's secretary went to look for a translator. When she came, the stewards presented their defence. Maria was sorry that she'd offended sister. She'd been angry, her back hurt and she'd lost her temper. She hadn't known the meaning of the English words she'd used. She heard English people using them when they were annoyed. She would never use the equivalent words in Spanish. And certainly not to sister.

Nobody actually believed this, but there was little management could do. Sister agreed to accept a translated apology and kept her mouth shut about previous English conversations with Maria. Management agreed to provide a bigger vacuum cleaner. The union regretted the incident.

This was a happy result. Usually, the stewards are not so inspired, the sister is not so forgiving and the manager is not so co-operative. Usually, what happens is the worker ends up with a warning, perhaps a final warning. Because, after all, she did do it.

The steward is in a cleft stick in these cases. The worker is rigid with rage and injustice. This is her whole life being judged here. It's her back and her work that's driving her crazy. And shouldn't be. The steward is sitting there trying to prove that she didn't say that. She bloody well felt it, and she had a right to say it. OK, so she shouldn't lose her temper. But she shouldn't lose her job, either. The steward isn't stating her case, speaking up for her life. He's just trying to save her job. He wants her to apologise. She'll be damned if she will. But at forty she needs the job. She apologises.

If the steward gets her off the hook she's grateful. But she doesn't feel that justice has been done. If she walks out of there with the threat of dismissal hanging over her head, she's angry with the steward. He's failed her, he couldn't argue, she needs the branch secretary instead of her stupid steward.

The steward is angry with her in turn. She's ungrateful. He risks his job and slogs his guts out every day and nobody even says thank you. This one ought to control her temper. That one keeps getting into trouble. And why can't that fool Costas do something about his timekeeping? Every time they get into trouble they come running to him. But when he asks them to do something, they look at him like he was a militant from Mars.

The steward knows it isn't down to him. After a successful strike the stewards can run rings around management. After a defeat, management keeps taking little bites out of conditions. If the workers in a section walk tall and stand by each other, the managers are careful and polite.

Hospital workers often don't really understand this. Many hospital workers have little experience of unions. A lot are immigrants from the countryside with little experience of unions at home. A lot are women who are the first generation of women in their families to belong to unions. Many hospital workers have never been on strike and are still teaching themselves about how unions work. At first, they see the power of the union as the personal property of the steward. It doesn't seem to come from daily struggles over line-speed and piecework. It seems to come because the steward is smart, argues well, and understands management and their world.

A big reason why hospital workers get this wrong is that stewards like to feel like little gods. As a steward, you know you're really only human. But when the grateful worker thanks you for getting her off, you smile a humble little smile . . . but you feel like a king. When you stand firm and argue loudly you know your 'member' is watching and admiring. (Indeed, it is often the worst stewards who argue the loudest. They're playing to the grandstand rather than trying to win the case.) You're proud of the little badge saying 'GMBATU steward' which the union gave you. You wear it everywhere. You drink with the other stewards in the pub and talk about 'my members'. You tell stories about how smart you are in negotiations. And if you take all the credit for the union, how can you avoid the blame?

Payslips

Let's turn to another example of the contradictions in the steward's position: negotiating over payslips. The weekly pay-slip is an incredibly complex document. It includes 5 per cent awards, special awards, lead-in payments, unconsolidated bonus, rostered overtime, casual overtime, rest-day working and much more. Each week the finance department makes a host of mistakes. Many workers take these mistakes to the steward to figure out. It's not that they can't understand the arithmetic. One of life's little miracles is that people who could never answer a maths problem in school can figure out overtime to the nearest penny with unfailing accuracy. It's more that they hate dealing with the finance department.

Few things anger a worker more than a false payslip. A personnel manager once explained to me that his years of experience had taught him that if you just got the payslips right, industrial relations would take care of themselves. He exaggerated, but he had a point.

It's like this. You work all day long at a job you hate. You give up your weekends with your family four years running for the overtime. You aren't respected, and the pay rates are a joke. At the end of it all, they don't even pay you what they agreed. What they're legally obliged to pay you. Half the time when you complain, the finance department tells you the computer made a mistake. Computers don't make mistakes, the people who feed them do. And why does the computer always make mistakes which *underpay* you? The only reason you work is the money, and now they're messing with the money and smirking at you when you complain. So you can't handle your anger and you go for the steward. Half the time the steward can't sort it out, either.

Take the case of a woman on the evening shift of cleaners. She wants to know why she's only got eighteen pounds left out of a gross of thirty. You take it to the finance department and they explain that this is a second job and they have to take the full tax. You tell her that, and she explodes in words and tears.

She says she's raising three kids on her own, the middle one is brain damaged and she has to take every Thursday off the other job to take him back and forth to the hospital, it's two buses and one of them is the 206, which you know never comes, and the kids needing things all the time, and it's OK getting somebody to look after the youngest and the oldest can look after himself, but it's hard to find anybody to look after the middle one – they always want more money – and she works, by God she works, she doesn't do two jobs for no reason, ever since he left she's had to work till her back ached and her heart bled for her babies. AND WHAT DO YOU MEAN THEY CAN'T GIVE ME THE MONEY I EARNED?

It's the tax law, you explain. Nobody can do anything about the Inland Revenue. I'm sorry. Here, have a hanky. Would you like a cup of tea? I'm sorry, I can't do anything.

With payslips, as with individual cases, sometimes you win and sometimes you lose. But you have to go by the book, and this produces tension between members and stewards. Yet it's just this tension which keeps the unions democratic. Stewards may usually be elected unopposed, but few people remain stewards if their members are unhappy with them. After all, they have to work and live together. If people keep complaining to the steward at the break and in the corridor and every time he turns around, the steward jacks it in. Or an unsatisfactory steward can simply be pushed to the margins. Demarcation lines between stewards are pretty fluid much of the time. If a porter doesn't think much of the porters' steward, he can usually go straight to the canteen steward. Or the porters can elect an additional steward and unload the bulk of the work onto him.

The unions

We turn now from the steward, and the problems that go with the job, to the unions themselves. This is a complicated subject, for there are many competing and overlapping unions. To simplify it, I'll start with a brief stereotype of each union. Then I'll move on to explain the thicket of personal animosity and historical accident which explains the actual pattern of union membership on the ground.

We'll begin with NUPE, the National Union of Public Employees. NUPE's members come about equally from local government manual workers and hospital ancillaries. The union is the descendant of the old London County Council manual workers' union. In the 1930s it grew by consistent recruiting among local authority workers, particularly road gangs and rubbish collectors. Given this background, it is concentrated in the hospitals among the ancillaries. The great majority of its hospital members are women, and almost half of them are part-timers.

NUPE has a reputation as a left-wing union. It's doubtful that the members are particularly left-wing themselves. In 1981, they were given a choice between Tony Benn and Denis Healey, as Deputy Leader of the Labour Party. They chose Healey, like everybody else. But ancillary workers are certainly the most combative section of hospital workers. The low pay of NUPE members has forced the leadership to oppose every pay policy, whether Labour or Tory. And that in turn has propelled the ancillaries into a series of struggles with the government.

Also, the NUPE officials are often on the left of the Labour Party. Almost all London full-timers, for instance, were active in support of Ken Livingstone and the Fares Fair campaign of 1982. These full-timers are active leftists, but not extremists. By and large, they are not drawn from the ranks of union activists. This is partly because unskilled manual workers used to have very little experience in trade unionism. Also, until 1972 the union was largely built through the skill of its officials in negotiating and arguing with council committees and management. Few NUPE activists had much experience of leading strikes, and negotiating skills seemed more important. So NUPE's first general secretary, for instance, was a former local official in the South Wales Miners' Federation. Its leader through the 1960s and 1970s was Alan Fisher, who began his working life as a clerk in the NUPE office and never left the union's employ. The present general secretary is Rodney Bickerstaffe. Like many NUPE full-timers, he is a graduate in sociology and from a working-class background. He went to work for the union right after leaving the Polytechnic. That was in 1969. Bickerstaffe is one of the cautious children of 1968 who has learned to work through the system. Like Fisher before him, his experience is bureaucratic. He's on the left of the Labour Party, but he's not at ease on a picket line.

COHSE is rather different. The letters stand for the Confederation of Health Service Employees, and it aspires to be the industrial union for the health service. COHSE is descended from an amalgamation of the old asylum attendants' union and the old Poor Law nurses' union. The asylum attendants, now transformed into psychiatric nurses, have usually been dominant. The mental hospitals are still COHSE's main base, and nursing unionism is far stronger there than elsewhere. The spirit of COHSE reflects the world of the mental nurse.

The majority of mental nurses are men. Usually, such a nurse came from the working class, worked hard in school, minded the teachers and passed his exams. He's intensely proud of his professional job, but he doesn't scorn or deny his origins. His job is both caring and authoritarian. The recruiting ad for mental nurses shows an understanding young man listening to a distressed woman. Before the invention of the pharmaceutical cosh, the old asylum attendants were recruited for their brawn to subdue wild patients. Nowadays, the mental nurse hovers between the two: at times, a careful and loving therapist; at times, almost a harassed and overworked gaoler.

This produces a tension which reinforces the mental nurse's urge towards respectability. And day by day he sees just what happens if you let yourself go. This strengthens the tight control which goes with the respectability. Many COHSE branch secretaries stand out at a conference of hospital workers. They're the middle-aged men in worn suits. They can't afford the casually expensive suits of the Medical Practitioners' Union. They're not about to go for the pseudo-proletarian heartiness of the NUPE jeans and open-necked shirt. COHSE is like these branch secretaries.

The full-timers are often drawn from the ranks of the activists, and they reflect the politics of their members. It's a cautious moderate union. COHSE does things by the book because it respects books and rules. Some COHSE full-timers seem instinctively frightened by the idea of strikes. And yet it's a real union – in many ways the most solidly based of all the hospital unions. The COHSE activist may be a moderate, but he hasn't forgotten he's a worker. He doesn't like things to get out of control, but he's bloody well not going to be pushed around.

NUPE and COHSE are the two big general unions. There are several other unions that organise in particular sections. ASTMS, for instance, the Association of Scientific, Technical and Managerial Staffs. Its general image is bustling, business-like and literate. Its main hospital base is among the lab technicians and kindred trades. It's a real union. Rarely is the branch secretary in management's pocket. But the members are largely moderate men and women with O-levels in hand and their eyes on a career structure. The essential moderation of many ASTMS branches, however, is camouflaged by the prevalence of left-wing stewards. Most of them owe their politics as much to ideas learned at college as to experience in the labour movement. They usually get along well with their members and some build a hotbed of militancy in their own section. Rarely are they able to build something wider.

NALGO is the National and Local Government Officers' Association. The name says it all. NALGO's big base is among white-collar council workers. There it has evolved over the last twenty years from a right-wing semi-union to a real union that mounts official strikes. In some areas a strong shop steward organisation has been built. In a few areas there have been long and bitter strikes by sections in NALGO. In the hospitals, NALGO is still where it was in local government in 1960.

It organises clerical and administrative grades. Management are union members. They can, and do, come to union meetings. This makes it difficult for any but the bravest to argue for militancy at union meetings. In some cases, the NALGO steward is in fact a junior member of management. The steward is usually a woman. In most cases she is a committed trade unionist. But she gets little support from her members and doesn't feel confident. This situation can change when a militant slowly builds up a strong branch over a period of years. However, many who might do that get fed up soon and switch over to NUPE or COHSE instead.

There are also specialist craft unions in the works department. The AUEW is for the engineers, EEPTU for the electricians and UCATT for the painters and carpenters. Some of these craft unions find themselves in a strong position in the larger hospitals. It's usually cheaper for management to buy off seven engineers than have them close the hospital by blacking the laundry boiler. But their sectional organisation makes them very vulnerable if management uses scabs or outside contractors. And UCATT is a weak union in the hospitals even when it has a strong steward. The carpenters and painters could be out for two years before management begin to panic.

There are other small craft unions in the hospitals: the Health Visitors' Association and the Medical Practitioners' Union. And there are the professional organisations, like the British Association of Occupational Therapists and the Chartered Society of Physiotherapists. They are not affiliated to the TUC. The most important of them is the Royal College of Nursing.

The RCN is the official face of nursing. It emphasises professionalism. It refuses to admit auxiliary nurses to its membership. Until recently, it was in favour of low wages for student nurses. After all, they were students and not workers. The RCN has a clause in its constitution which forbids strikes. This clause has regularly been upheld by conferences and ballots of the membership.

The RCN is the majority organisation among trained nurses in the larger general hospitals. But since NUPE and COHSE have the auxiliaries and COHSE a lot of the mental nurses, the TUC unions outnumber the RCN among nurses as a whole.

Union militants, particularly nursing militants, get apoplectic over the RCN. They say it's dominated by sisters and management, relentlessly respectable and elitist and all too willing to sell out conditions. All this is true. But under pressure from its members and TUC competition, the RCN has felt obliged to edge towards trade unionism. It's now registered with the government as a union. But it still resolutely refuses to affiliate to the TUC like the great unwashed masses of social workers, finance officers, university lecturers and tax inspectors. The RCN has stewards like other unions. By and large they are not much use, since the nurses of an appropriate turn of mind tend to join a TUC union. The RCN is still, in the minds of most nurses, what you join if you want a union but don't want to be forced into striking and betraying your patients.

Union membership

The large number of hospital unions may seem a bit confusing. But the reality in any one hospital is more confusing still, since so many workers don't belong to the union they 'ought' to belong to. In a small hospital, one of the specialist unions may lack anybody brave or foolish enough to be a steward. People work in such small departments that they make work-friends outside their section. Lacking their own steward, they join their friends' union.

Also, many hospital unions were built up by workers with experience in other industries. They came into the health service and were appalled at what they saw. So they recruited everybody into their own union. Some port cities have TGWU hospitals built by ex-dockers. Some ambulance stations are TGWU because of the workers who are ex-lorry drivers. There are general hospitals where a nurse from the old Poor Law hospitals recruited everyone into COHSE, and so on.

But the main reason for the confused pattern of union membership today is the past theft of union members. Many years ago, a TUC meeting in Bridlington reached agreement on the practice of signing up another union's members. The 'Bridlington agreement' said you couldn't do it. In many industries today you speak solemnly of 'invoking Bridlington' if somebody tries it. In the hospitals it's a free for all. As far as hospital workers and their union officials are concerned, Bridlington is a small town on the coast of Yorkshire. If a group of workers get fed up with the way their NUPE full-timer is handling their claim, off they go to COHSE. If the COHSE branch secretary crosses a picket line, half his members decamp to the TGWU. And so on, endlessly. The result is a pattern of union membership which is a consequence of animosities and personal followings now long forgotten.

Two detailed examples will show the patchwork-quilt nature of union membership. First take St Catherine's, a small 200-bed hospital. Here all the cleaners were in NUPE, but less than half the porters. The other half had recently followed their steward into the GMBATU. He said that NUPE was being manipulated by a communist branch secretary. They were just mad militants who didn't care about the workers. Privately, he said that the GMBATU was an English union. NUPE responded with a whispering campaign that the GMBATU was in the head porter's pocket and the steward was a racist. The porters weighed up these claims and wavered back and forth.

The GMBATU, meanwhile, was busy recruiting among the clerical staff who were annoyed because their steward, a works manager, wasn't doing anything for them. The steward himself was just holding down the job out of loyalty to the union and fond memories of the time he was a young man in UCATT.

The works department themselves used to be in NUPE. But the union hadn't supported them in a strike. One of them had been in the AUEW in a lot of factories. He remembered it as a lot better than this shower. He recruited his mates into the AUEW on the grounds that it was a craft union for tradesmen like themselves, not slobs like porters. But one engineer remained in NUPE, by agreement between NUPE and the AUEW. The AUEW steward and the NUPE chair were drinking buddies, and this lone member justified them negotiating together over works department matters. And when the AUEW steward couldn't make his union's stewards meetings, the NUPE chair went as a substitute.

The situation in the kitchen was ticklish. The head chef was a strong GMBATU man. The kitchen porters were Sicilians. They were split between those who joined NUPE because they remembered how much they hated the landlord and those who joined the GMBATU because they remembered how much they feared the landlord. Their political differences were not as bitter as the ones the Spanish porters had over King Juan Carlos, however. The royalists were in the GMBATU, the left in NUPE.

The canteen workers were a moderate lot, and inclined towards the head chef and the GMBATU. But the AUEW steward was the boyfriend of one of the canteen workers, and he persuaded her mates to stay in NUPE.

This is a simple example in a small hospital. Let's look at another hospital of similar size. Here most of the ancillaries were in NUPE. But most of the porters were fed up with NUPE and belonged to nothing. The physiotherapists were in their chartered society, and the occupational therapists in their association. The pharmacy workers were almost all in ASTMS, but had no steward. One woman in the pharmacy was in NUPE, as was one woman from the general office. The other woman in the general office was in NALGO with the medical records staff. The NUPE secretary had been in NALGO herself since she was a secretary by trade, but she'd got fed up and joined NUPE. She ran it together with the laundry supervisor, who had been steward for the domestics for years. The lone carpenter was in UCATT but went to NUPE meetings. The engineers were split between the AUEW and NUPE – one each.

The majority of the nurses were in NUPE, but some sisters were in NALGO because they felt it was a white-collar union. Sixty nurses belonged to the COHSE branch in a neighbouring hospital. They were mostly on nights, where there was a COHSE steward who had originally worked in the neighbouring hospital. Six nurses were in the TGWU. They had transferred from another hospital where the union activist happened to have a brother who was a full-time official in the TGWU. At the time of the transfer, the NUPE laundry supervisor agreed to represent them without seducing them over to NUPE.

Shop stewards' committees

Remember that these are simple examples from small hospitals. The picture is much more complicated in a big general hospital three times the size. And the thicket of unions is really dense in a large health district. Imagine the problems of organising a district shop stewards' committee.

Take the example of the West Burton district shop stewards' committee. The West Burton health district covers five hospitals: one large teaching hospital, a mental hospital, a middle-sized general hospital, a geriatric hospital and a small specialist hospital. The district has a unified management who plot together. There is one big district laundry, a district stores and a district transport and a district finance section. On most important issues the stewards find themselves confronting a unified management. The need for a joint shop stewards' committee (JSSC) is obvious. Everybody agrees it's a good idea. But . . .

The first problem is where and when to start. Management

refuse time off with pay for stewards' meetings. They cite a DHSS directive which says stewards can only have paid time off to handle members' cases. But of course management are not unaware of the threat of a strong JSSC.

The obvious solution is to hold meetings after work. Only half the nurses finish at four and the other half at ten. Clerks and technicians are off at five, but the works staff have an hour of regular overtime till six. The cleaners have always finished at four so they can pick up their kids at school. Except for the evening cleaners, who leave the kids with the husband and work five to eight. The catering staff start very early and finish by three, though the supper shift stays till eight or nine.

Somewhat over half the stewards are women. Even if they don't have to get home for the kids, their husbands expect dinner on the table by six. Right after work is the hardest time for them to make. But by eight at night they're just too tired to go out again.

So the West Burton JSSC meets in the lunch break. That way nobody loses any money. Fine. Whose lunch hour? The white-collar workers take theirs at one and the manuals at twelve. This is in accordance with ancient class distinctions whose meaning is lost in the mists of time. The cleaners complicate things by only getting half-an-hour. This is part of the deal which lets them get away early in the afternoon. Catering can't take a break during lunch and the nurses and porters have to stagger their breaks so the job is covered. Cleaners and nurses have a day off in the week to make up for working weekends, so on any given day some of them are missing.

A class compromise means the meetings start at 12.30 and last an hour. Lots of people have to come late and lots of others leave early. Some people try to stay the whole meeting and sit there feeling itchy about what the supervisor is going to say when they're forty-five minutes late from lunch. Some people just decide to miss the hour and have an hour's *overtime* docked.

The meetings are at the teaching hospital, since it's the biggest. It's fifteen to thirty minutes in different directions to the smaller hospitals. By the time the mental hospital stewards get to the meeting, they have to turn around and go back.

The people who come late want to repeat what everybody else has already said. You've only got an hour and there's an important strike in the specialist hospital. But the jerk from transport uses up twenty minutes with his aggressive confusion about London weighting allowances. Then the NUPE stewards decide to have a go at their branch secretary. They use up thirty minutes being angry, and everyone else is bored and irritated. There's ten minutes left to discuss a critical strike, and half the stewards have left already. Most of them felt disgruntled.

The attendance varies from meeting to meeting. There are a few regulars. Four trotskyists are willing to lose the money out of political passion. One of them writes articles for *Socialist Worker* and proudly signs them 'Secretary, West Burton JSSC'. There's a right-winger from works whose boss couldn't care less what he does. There are three NUPE branch officials. They've worked themselves into positions where they can take unlimited time off and management doesn't ask questions. But when it comes to taking action, you miss the laundry steward and the porters' steward. They've got the best-organised sections and will lead anything that counts. Management know that and have nailed their feet to the ground. They can rarely get to meetings.

There are a lot of practical difficulties in organising the JSSC. Many of them spring from the weakness of the JSSC itself. A strong JSSC could insist on time off and proper meetings. But how do you build that strong committee in the first place with divided unions and a divided workforce?

For the JSSC's greatest handicap is the heritage of inter-union rivalry and member-snatching. This NUPE branch secretary and his COHSE opposite number hate each other from way back. There's also a tradition of scabbing. NUPE crosses COHSE picket lines, nurses walk past porters, porters sidle past catering, the mental hospital stays in while the teaching hospital joins a national one-day strike. It feels lonely watching somebody cross your picket line. People don't forget.

There are personal rivalries too. One NUPE steward ran against the branch secretary last year, and they're barely speaking. The NALGO branch secretary is livid with the NALGO steward who took a day's sick leave during the one-day strike. She's also a bit leery of the NUPE clerical steward who recruited four of her members last week. And so on.

Another basic difficulty is the split between manual and white-collar stewards. This split always looms when action is discussed. The manual workers are usually better organised and far more likely to actually go out the door. In a factory, this greater militancy usually goes hand in hand with numbers on the stewards' committee. The AUEW, say, will be the dominant union among the workers and among the stewards. But in a hospital the manual workers are a bare majority of the workforce. They rarely have a clear majority of stewards on the JSSC. The story doesn't end there, though. The manual workers still make up the majority of *union members* and the great majority of strikers. So when push comes to shove, votes in the JSSC don't mean all that much.

There's considerable strangled resentment and embarrassment about this split in the committee. It's doubled and redoubled by the daily jealousies and hierarchies of hospital life. A NUPE porter is regularly insulted and snubbed by nurses or medical records staff in the course of his work. When the portering steward deals with nursing and clerical stewards in the JSSC, he has to keep reminding himself that these people are serious trade unionists. (His unspoken qualification is 'unlike their members'.) As soon as there is a dispute in the JSSC, he stops reminding himself.

Another difficulty is that many of the stewards at the meetings don't have much confidence in their members or feeling of their own power. They come to the JSSC partly to get a feeling of the collective power. They find themselves in a room with people who mostly want to feel the same thing but don't feel confident either. Their demands are high: it's no wonder they often come away feeling frustrated.

The West Burton JSSC has a lot of problems. Yet it is an outstandingly successful district committee as these things go. It actually does discuss disputes and raise money and sometimes tries to organise strikes. But, first and foremost, it exists. The same sort of difficulties that hinder the West Burton JSSC make stewards' committees impossible in most districts. In fact, there are no joint union committees in the individual hospitals in West Burton district either. Personal rivalries and sectional antagonisms can be submerged at a big district meeting. Within each hospital, the feelings have been too bitter too long.

Union leaders

Of course, many hospitals have stewards' committees within each individual union. But for most hospitals these are not the main form of union organisation. The local unions are largely built around a few local chiefs.

In most cases, these chiefs are the informal leaders of the larger manual unions. Often the chief is the branch secretary, but not always. Sometimes he's* the branch chair. In other cases one steward may be the leader within one hospital, while the branch secretary works at another site. The union positions are usually just a formal recognition of informal followings. Leadership is personal.

The chief builds a personal following through negotiation and advice to stewards. For instance, a nursing steward is faced with a tricky case. Her member has four weeks' holiday coming to her at Christmas. She applies for an extra two weeks' unpaid leave so she can take six weeks and visit the West Indian island where she was born but hasn't seen for eighteen years. She assumes her request for unpaid leave will be granted and books a charter ticket. Leave is denied. The steward gets nowhere with nursing management. Matron says she can't spare anybody. She's within her rights: unpaid leave is discretionary. It's obviously unjust, but the steward doesn't know what to do. So she calls up somebody more senior in the union hierarchy whom she thinks can handle it. He takes it up, negotiates well, and the nurse gets her leave.

This sort of thing happens again and again. The stewards gradually develop a loyalty to certain good negotiators. They go to these men constantly for advice and experience. The demand for people with confidence and brains is insatiable. Most stewards

---

*I am using the male pronoun to reflect the crucial realities of hospital life. Most branch secretaries are men and most NALGO stewards are women – and this has a critical effect on the way they work with one another.

don't feel stupid. By and large, they know they're pretty smart. But they feel shaky with higher management and very nervous when they are negotiating anything that's critical to their members. A lot of the union chief's job is simply 'pumping up' anxious stewards. It's a wearing and demanding task.

In some hospitals, there is only one chief. In many hospitals, two or three people gladly share the load between them. In many small hospitals no one wants to be union chief at all. Traditionally, the stewards in such hospitals have turned to the union full-timer to be their negotiator and adviser. But, more and more, a respected union chief will take on two or three small hospitals in addition to his own. Many union chiefs are ambitious men, and they get great satisfaction from being able to help increase the powers of their class. Some also get more money by taking on more hospitals. In NUPE, branch secretaries get one-eighth of their members' dues. It's no wonder many NUPE branches just seem to grow and grow.

These union chiefs obviously have to take a lot of time off for union duties. A few are full-time convenors who do nothing but union work and have an office and desk of their own in the hospital. Most have a more informal arrangement whereby they are allowed time off for union business when they need it, and they need it a lot of the time. In any case, only people in certain sorts of jobs can be active leaders. A good job is something like porter in a big hospital. There are thirty other porters in the pool and they can cover you easily. Nobody gets upset if you go off. The next best thing is a job where you work largely on your own. Then you rush through your work, rush through the union work, and rush back to stay late and finish the work that has piled up. Best of all is to get a job where management doesn't expect you to do too much. Deputy-head porter and security man can both be turned into this kind of job. The worst sort of job is one where you work in a small section, with two or three people who have to cover for you. People in this position often become stewards, but hardly ever leaders.

Taking time off depends on your power, your position and management's feelings about you. The branch secretary in a militant and confident branch simply tells his supervisor he's going off on union business. And a union leader is also in a strong position if management know he's a moderate who might be replaced by a crazed trotskyist if they're not careful.

In many people's minds, the union leader is the union personified. He may in fact have built the union in that particular hospital up from nothing. And many hospital workers have never worked in any other industry and never been on strike for more than a day. They see the union largely as a form of insurance, rather than as a tool of collective action. And they see the stewards and the chief as the union. So it's possible to walk into most hospitals and say to the first ancillary you see: 'Who's the union here?' They'll take you to see Bill or Steve or whoever. Again, hospital workers often say, 'I don't like the union. Bill never did anything on my accident case.'

The union chief is usually a man. Most of his members are women. The largest section among them are the cleaners. Some union leaders behave almost like supervisors with their cleaners' steward. Some behave like kindly uncles. In both cases the stewards tell him how the members feel and what they will and will not do. He advises them what they can do in the union and supports them in negotiation. It's a paternalist relationship.

I should emphasise that this paternalism is found in many different sorts of union chiefs. It's built into the job. It characterises right-wing branch secretaries who refuse to hold union meetings and call their stewards 'my girls'. It also characterises the trotskyist branch secretary with a sophisticated understanding of sexism who always goes on abortion demos. The style may differ, but the dependence remains. Not that the relationship between stewards and leader is usually hostile. The imbalance is produced not by the sexism or bossiness of any one union leader (though these may enter in). Rather, it's produced by a whole sexist society. Men don't take women seriously, and women are raised not to take themselves seriously. Remember that the root of the chief's position is the weakness of the stewards' committees and the shakiness of the individual steward. That shakiness can turn to power. In recent years, women have become union chiefs. But it takes time and it runs against the grain of the whole society. Man or woman, powerful forces push any union chief towards moderation.

Of course, many union chiefs have achieved their present position through years of struggle. They have worked conscientiously on members' cases and led strikes. And they depend on the members to back them up when management threatens. The union chief who is not a serious trade unionist is common enough, but he's in a minority. Most have a constant eye out for the good of the working class and the state of their organisation this week.

Still, they do spend most of their time on individual cases. They have the same problems as the other stewards, only writ larger. They are usually called in on the hard cases: particularly the unwinnable ones. They, too, need a good working relationship with management. This helps in negotiations. They also need management's co-operation to get them time off for union duties. A strong and vindictive management can ground them. And the leader needs management not to hate him so much that they sack him. Most cases of victimisation in the hospitals have been lost in the last few years. Union leaders are well aware of these cases.

Inevitably, union leaders start to feel resentful about disputes. For the individual steward, a strike in her department can be the high point in her life. For the branch secretary covering five hospitals, the first strike against the cuts is welcome. The fourth is exhausting. The sixth time he has to give up his evenings and keep taking stomach pills, the feeling is, 'Oh no, not again.'

Fear of losing his job or wrecking the union organisation plays on the mind of any union chief. He's usually enormously proud of what he's built and feels it's for the good of the class. Also, it's a lot more fun being a union branch secretary and going to meetings than it is being a porter and humping tables. You are an important and respected person, not 'just a porter'. The idea of returning to being a nothing can be terrifying.

In NUPE it can also involve considerable financial loss. The branch secretary of a large NUPE branch may be getting an extra £50 or £60 a week from his share of the dues. He will have built not just his holiday plans but his mortgage around that.

The pressures towards moderation operate on both right-wing

leaders and leftists. Some may be more concerned with the consequences for the class of a serious defeat. Some may be more concerned with their standing in the local labour movement or their political party. But all are subject to the same pressures that make full-timers such a conservative force. After all, they are doing largely the same job as the full-timers.

But there are two big differences between full-timers and leaders. One is that the full-time official can afford to lose a strike. He will be sad and bitter. But he won't lose his job and he won't have to live in the wreckage of a union. So the union chiefs are likely to be cautious about strikes. But once they're out the gate, they are desperate to win. They have more to lose than anybody else. The union full-timer will be under pressure from his head office to settle.

The full-timer, after all, is appointed by the union hierarchy. His hopes of a career and his working life depend on them. The union leader is responsible to the stewards and the members. He comes under enormous pressure from them if they think he is selling out. He has to live with them. That's one of the reasons union leaders remain as militant as they do. The other is that they are often men or women with years of struggle and principle behind them.

Only a few union chiefs are corrupt. The man who sticks his hand in the till is a fool, though there is the occasional fool. He can make himself a good deal more, safely, by taking his legitimate cut out of the dues and getting management to give him an extra hour's overtime a day. He spends it sitting in his office. This isn't exactly corruption, but it's something a union chief will fight hard to hold on to. It's very difficult to remove such a 'militantly moderate' union chief. He can refuse to hold stewards' meetings or mass meetings. He can hold the annual general meeting on a Sunday in a pub. He can expel from the union any steward who looks like a threat.

At the height of a strike you can get rid of that type in twenty-four hours flat. Otherwise, the stewards just have to go round him. The stewards look to other branch officers to help with their cases. The stewards in other hospitals in the branch strike out on their own more or call in the full-timer more. In some cases they go off and join another branch or another union.

But most leaders have the respect of their stewards. They are the lynch-pin of the union at local level. Their strength reflects the weakness of the stewards. These in turn reflect weakness and disunity among the workers themselves. The pressures towards moderation and routine may be severe for union leaders. But that's not because they're bad men or weak. I've been a union chief myself and I'm proud of it.

Whitley councils

We turn now from the hurly-burly of the shop floor to the distasteful subject of the workings of the unions at national level. Here, most energy is concentrated on the 'Whitley council' system. These councils were originally designed by a man named Whitley, during the first world war, a time of national crisis. The idea was that there would be two equal sides to every council. Management would have half the seats and the union the other half. Together they would negotiate and fix national agreements on pay and conditions. Co-operation would replace strikes and conflict. A turbulent labour movement would be appeased and tamed so that production would flow smoothly and the blood-bath could continue. The patriotic unions duly entered these councils. After the war, the weaker unions were stuck with them.

These days, there are eleven Whitley councils in the NHS. One covers general matters, like payments for car mileage and union stewards' facilities. Ten councils cover different sections of the workforce. The two most important are the ancillaries' council and the nurses' and midwives' council. We will look at each in turn.

There are sixteen staff-side seats on the ancillary council. NUPE has four, COHSE four, the TGWU four and the GMBATU four. This does not remotely reflect the actual membership on the ground. NUPE has over half the ancillaries and COHSE most of the rest. The GMBATU and the TGWU have only small pockets among the ancillaries.

Moreover, the other three unions all tend to be more inclined to settle with management than NUPE. COHSE is traditionally a more moderate union. The general unions are nationally un-responsive to their health service members. If you're a builder or a lorry driver in the TGWU then you have an influential trade group in the union. But if you're a hospital worker, your full-timer often knows little of the industry and the national leader-ship doesn't feel under any pressure to care. For instance, when the Callaghan government brought the cuts to the NHS, NUPE and COHSE objected. Their leaders were compelled to do so by the feeling on the ground. TGWU and GMBATU members felt just as strongly, but their union leaders felt safe in supporting the cuts as part of a strategy to save British industry. (I know it sounds ridiculous now, but at the time people thought that was a serious argument.)

So year after year the following charade takes place on the ancillaries' council. The unions receive an offer on ancillaries' pay. They consult the members. The members reject the offer. The employers refuse to increase it. The alternative is a strike. So COHSE, the TGWU and the GMBATU vote in a staff-side meeting to accept. NUPE votes against accepting the offer, secure in the knowledge that their principled stand won't make any difference. The offer is accepted. NUPE officials tell their stewards and members that they didn't want to accept that awful deal. But the other unions outvoted them, the useless wankers. The NUPE officials quietly suggest that the stewards go out and steal members from the useless unions who sign such deals. This the stewards do. NUPE grows.

This is called the 'NUPE trick'. It can be used on anything, not just on pay negotiations. It drives the national officials of the other unions to distraction. They *know* that the NUPE leader-ship have no more intention than they do of actually doing anything. But they daren't actually say so in public. So usually they just gnash their teeth in private.

NUPE stewards tend to misunderstand the 'NUPE trick'. They blame what happens on the Whitley system. You can raise a heart-felt cheer at any NUPE stewards' meeting by calling for the destruction of the Whitley council. Of course, NUPE never does actually resign from the council. Even being on the council, NUPE still has the members and the strength to strike on their own. Whitleyism doesn't prevent NUPE being militant, it just makes possible the 'NUPE trick'.

Mind you, the ancillaries' council hasn't been useless over the years. The unions have gradually won a whole series of overtime rates: night-work payments, rotary shifts, alternating shifts, rest-day payments, unsocial hours payments, on-call payments, payments for acting up to a higher grade, and so on. These have made considerable difference to gross pay. For instance, if you work Saturday night you get time-and-a-half for overtime and an extra one-fifth for night work on top of that.

During the years of the long boom, management didn't mind too much conceding these rates. Management had trouble finding people to do such low paid jobs with no prestige and such awful hours. Then, when bad times came in the 1970s, management were stuck with their earlier agreements. They had already been enshrined in the red Whitley council handbook that personnel managers and branch secretaries treated as a bible.

These decent rates particularly benefited men's jobs. Porters were the big gainers. It is they who do the most shift work and nights. It's not entirely coincidental that porters have often been the backbone of hospital unions and that so many branch secretaries are porters.

Of course, women got benefits too. Most cleaners and canteen staff work weekends, and the rates made a major difference to them. But the ancillaries' council has never responded to requests to eliminate the bottom two grades. These grades cover almost all women cleaners and canteen staff. They cover almost no men.

But at least the ancillaries' council has done more than the nurses' and midwives' council. The list below gives the distribution of seats on the nurses' staff side.

COHSE	4
NUPE	4
NALGO	2
GMBATU	1
Health Visitors' Association	2
Scottish Health Visitors' Association	1
TUC unions, total seats	**14**

Association of Nurse Administrators*	1
Association of Hospitals and Residential Care Officers	1
Royal College of Midwives	3
Royal College of Nursing	8
Scottish Association of Nurse Administrators*	1
Association of Supervisors of Midwives*	1
Professional associations, total seats	**15**

Final score: unions 14, rest of the world 15

Here again the seats do not reflect membership on the ground. The professional associations have a majority on the council. They largely follow the lead of the RCN, which is thus able to set the tone of the council. And note that three small associations of managers (marked with an asterisk) appear to occupy seats on the 'staff side'.

This has enabled the unions to blame the council's failure on the RCN. These failures are severe. Overtime is paid at time-and-a-quarter. Night work is paid at time-and-a-quarter. The two cannnot be added together, so Saturday night is time-and-a-quarter. Sundays are time-and-a-half. If forced to work outside rostered hours at short notice you don't necessarily get overtime. Management can simply choose to lay you off for one of the days you were supposed to work. In fact, many nurses are forbidden overtime in their own hospital. That hospital simultaneously employs moonlighting agency nurses who work full-time at another hospital. All this means that a nurse working the same shifts as a porter and earning the same basic wages is likely to gross about two-thirds of what the porter makes.

No other job in Britain has such lousy overtime and shift rates. And the great majority of nurses work shifts and weekends. Nurses are a large proportion of the hospital workforce, and it would be very expensive for the NHS to pay proper rates. The nurses' council hasn't pushed them.

Here, all the TUC unions work the 'NUPE trick'. They blame everything on the RCN. Of course, any Monday morning they chose they could ignore the council and refuse to accept the RCN's dictates, since they have a majority of members. But if they did so they would then have nobody to blame but themselves. So they stay on the council.

The nursing council is particularly bad on the bottom grades. The wage deals usually involve not just more money for tutors and administrators, but larger percentage increases. The RCN says straight out that auxiliaries and student nurses should be paid less than other people.

These two councils are the most important. They give an idea of some of the problems with Whitleyism. But the biggest problem of all is that you just can't get your hands on the system. The fire brigades, for instance, have one union with one set of negotiators. This means that the national negotiators are at least partly responsible to the union members through the annual conference. It was only because they were so responsible that the fire service was able to go on strike in 1978. The NHS system, by contrast, is so complex that negotiators are effectively responsible to nobody. Individual unions ballot their members when, and if, they feel like it. Until 1982 no wage offers were ever presented to a union conference. Wage deals can be, and are, settled against the express wish of the majority of the workers.

On non-wage matters there are few effective lines between the local unions and the councils. Say George, the NUPE steward, is concerned about the grading of plaster technicians or night rates for nurses. He wants to bring the matter to the attention of the national negotiators. He takes it to his district stewards' meeting. They send it to the area stewards who send it to the divisional committee or the national NHS committee. They tell the NUPE negotiators, who tell the other Whitley unions about it. Somebody writes a polite letter to the plaster technicians' steward and files it. The force of the stewards' concern is lost somewhere along the line. Some of the bodies that consider his motion only meet quarterly, after all. It takes an awful lot of letters and resolutions before anybody does anything.

National leaders

The union leaders at a national level spend most of their time enmeshed in Whitley councils. The local officials spend their time negotiating individual cases and bonus schemes. They are intimately concerned in all strikes in their area. The national officials, by contrast, are removed from the shop floor. I have stood on many picket lines, and I've never seen an area or national official on one.

This is part of the reason that national officials tend to be so conservative when it comes to taking action. The rank-and-file ancillaries usually think this is simply because the officials are doing all right for themselves. They have fat salaries, good mortgages and company cars. Why should they care about low pay?

It's true enough that the general secretary of NALGO, for instance, makes £51,000 a year basic. The constant round of bureaucratic meetings does mean that the national leaders tend to soak up some of the world view of the other men with briefcases. The forces that push them to the right are not counterbalanced by the exposure to stewards and members which keeps a branch secretary in line.

But they're not to the right of their members politically. For instance, in 1981 the entire leadership of NUPE supported Tony Benn for Deputy Leader of the Labour Party. They put the question to their members, who voted decisively for Healey.

NUPE is perhaps the most left wing of the hospital unions. But the pattern is general and characteristic of almost all British unions. The union apparatus is usually to the left of the membership until it comes to action. This can be traced to a fundamental contradiction in the consciousness of the British working class.

On the one hand, British workers are quite right wing in their general political attitudes. One-third traditionally vote Tory. A majority probably support some sort of right-wing Labour position. But when it comes to their own political circumstances British workers are often very militant. This has been the rock on which every pay policy has foundered. The opinion polls regularly reveal that unionised workers support wage control. At the same time each group of workers feels it is wildly unfair to apply that pay policy in their own case. They can see that they themselves don't have enough money for the essentials. Pay policy applies to the workers who earn a bundle and do almost no work, like the British Leyland workers you read about in the papers. It doesn't apply to me.

 This contradiction between politics and militancy has deep historical roots. For a century and a half Britain was the world's leading imperial power. After the second world war there was a twenty-year boom. In the long run it seemed that capitalism did deliver the goods. So at a national level you didn't rock the boat or hope for revolution. At the same time, you needed strong and active shop stewards to make sure that you got your share of the cake. So you elected a communist as convenor because he was a strong militant trade unionist. You elected a right winger as national secretary because you were no communist yourself. This produced a notable paradox. Britain had the best organised working class in the world, with a strong sense of itself as a class. At the same time it was the only country in Europe without a significant communist party.

 Until recently British workers could live comfortably enough with militant leaders on the ground and moderate leaders in head office. There was enough money for the ruling class to concede something to the militants without threatening the whole system. Nowadays, there is no such leeway for the employers. The contradictions in workers' heads become critical. Their local militancy leads them into struggle and their general political moderation makes them elect leaders who will lose that struggle. This confusion at ground level is lived out as a tension between leaders and rank and file.

The impact of feminism

Let us turn now from the depressing world of the Whitley councils to some of the changes that have been happening in the rank and file. One of the most important has been the effect of feminism upon hospital workers. In a way, feminism is the wrong word for what I want to describe. In Britain, clear feminist politics has been largely confined within parts of the middle class. Not that feminism is inherently 'middle class'. In the USA tens of millions of working-class women see themselves as feminists. In Britain, for various reasons, this has not yet happened. But there has been a massive, slow and tentative change in the way women see themselves in the world. It's something larger than political feminism. It's also something that couldn't have happened without feminism. The key phrase is 'I'm no bra burner, but . . .' The emphasis is on the *but*.

The position of women in hospital unions has been changing. Women hospital unionists have never been just the same as men. Men vote for or against strikes. If they vote for, they go out and slog away on picket lines together. Win or lose, back they come.

Women, on the other hand, tend to be either the best militants or the worst scabs. They used to be the unorganised and conservative sections. But once action starts, it is the cleaners who form the backbone. They vote most strongly to come out. They stand on picket lines and go on demonstrations while the men spend the day of the strike in bed or down the pub.

This volatility stems from the subjection of women. Historically, they followed where the union led, but strikes and conflict were the work of men. Passive conservatism was the product of their subjection. Yet once they actually got out the door the release was intoxicating. When a woman goes on strike for the first time she rejects the latest pay offer. But she also rejects her own idea of what it is to be a woman.

A picket line of women on strike for the first time is a good place to be. Faces are wreathed in happiness. Joy bubbles. For that day, it doesn't matter if they win or lose the dispute. What matters to Thelma is that she finally got up and walked out that door.

Men are likely to make more practical calculations. They look at how much they are losing on strike and what they feel the deal on offer is likely to give them. The women are more likely to want to hang on to their new understanding of themselves.

Of course, the differences between men and women are not cut and dried. In a long strike men, too, develop a new pride and a fierce loyalty to one another. And things are often different for women if their husbands are out of work or if they're single mothers. Then the same worries about producing the rent and housekeeping money that torment the men creep into their minds. They, too, become pragmatic.

It's not that women's incomes are unnecessary frills and men's wages critical. It takes two wages to support a working-class family. Rather, it's that most working men see their central job as *supporting* their families. Most working women see their central job as *caring* for their families. Both are deluded. Children need fathers just as much as women need money. But that's how most people feel. So the man goes on strike to protect his central function: earning a decent wage. He is driven back to work by guilt when he can't put food on his children's plates. A woman refrains from striking because it isn't her business. She stays out on strike because it's a breath of fresh air in a small stale room.

In the last ten years many women have been on strike in the hospitals. Often, it's only been for a day. But that day has changed their view of themselves. Until then, a woman has always let somebody else negotiate for her. Now, on the picket line, she feels like an active trade unionist. She stands there all day. She argues with people why they shouldn't cross. She walks up to a lorry, tentatively, and the driver listens to her and turns his enormous rig away. She collects money and organises getting the tea. She makes placards out of old cardboard boxes and does the lettering herself. Next time something starts happening, she turns up in the branch secretary's office and asks what she can do. He gets her elected steward fast.

At first she's a very hesitant steward. If she's a domestic she feels reasonably confident taking up grievances with the domestic supervisor. The supervisor is a working-class woman, too. She's got more power than the steward, but there's nothing scary or mysterious about her. Dealing with higher management is different. She feels out of her depth with the men with the ties behind the desks. She calls in the union chief or the full-timer. They take her into the negotiations with them. But she isn't in charge of the strategy. At some point in the talking, she'll blurt out her angry feelings. But she's not eyeing the management and calculating her words, looking for advantage and measuring her backing among the members. She's representing her members. She hasn't made the jump to leading them.

Many women and men stewards never make that jump. After all, good leaders don't grow on trees. But increasingly more women have begun to see themselves as leaders. They owe this, more or less consciously, to feminism. Many feminist ideas have been contained, but the idea that women are as good as men is now in surprisingly wide circulation. They also owe it to their own activity. When nothing much is happening, the negotiators seem the best people to run the union. When action starts it's the women arguing on picket lines and in the mess rooms who see themselves as the union.

Take the example of St Gilbert's. As in many hospitals, the union had long been run by a couple of porters. Then half the wards were threatened with closure. Two women threw themselves into the fight to save the hospital. They devoted themselves to organising an occupation. They spoke at meetings almost every night of the week. They taught themselves to write leaflets. Their sheer anger over what was happening to the hospital they loved propelled them into management's office. It kept them yelling and jeering once they got in there.

They lost the campaign. They won the respect of the workers in the hospital. Within two years, one of them was branch chair and the other assistant branch secretary. The porters who had run the union were now on the margins. Bitter, they dropped out of the union altogether.

Note that neither of the women became branch secretary. There was a sitting branch secretary at a neighbouring hospital. He was a powerful and determined man. It's always difficult to remove a branch secretary, and they didn't want to. But within four years the union moved from having an all-male leadership to having a mostly female one.

This sort of change has happened in fits and starts in many hospitals. It's not really possible to document it statistically. After all, there have always been women stewards and women branch officers. What's changing is that more of them are seeing themselves as leaders rather than sidekicks. For example, in both 1976 and 1982 I went around hospitals in East London looking for people who could organise collections and support for a strike. In 1976, most of the union leaders were men. In 1982, about half the people who could actually get things done were women. Many of the branch secretaries were the same people as before. But there were new women leaders in many of the small hospitals.

The rise of women leaders has important effects. For the glory of the British trade unions is the shop steward system. Aside from Ireland and Australia, there's nothing like it anywhere else in the world. The strength of this system is in its roots. The negotiators for the workers are also people up to their necks in a working life. When the class feels weak, they feel frightened. When the class feels aggressive, they feel jubilant. They talk the language of the workers because it's their language. By and large, their members trust them.

You see the strength of the steward system clearly when the stewards decide their members should strike over something. They start talking with their members. They talk endlessly in the canteens, on the wards and in the mess rooms. They argue, cajole, encourage and bore their members. They build towards a mass meeting. The full-time official and a few stewards speak at the meeting. The full-timer often speaks well and sometimes eloquently. The members listen politely. The stewards often don't speak well, though God knows they try. They're sweating with nerves before the meeting. Often they're so gripped by fear and hope they can hardly put words straight. A woman steward gets stuck in the middle of her prepared speech. She looks around the room. Then she just says what she feels in a rush of emotion. She's the one who convinces the meeting.

The members know their steward. They have observed her weaknesses. They respect her honesty. They know she's one of them. Bill from the kitchen gets up at the meeting and starts going on about how they shouldn't strike because it will put their jobs in danger. The kitchen steward leaps up and shouts at Bill that if it were up to him they'd never do anything but what Mr Owens says. Everybody laughs. They know she's right.

The stewards are a great strength of the union. And the union is stronger when women stewards lead it. Not because women are smarter or more left wing or more sensitive. Some are, some aren't. But because most hospital workers are women. Without strong women stewards the domestics don't really get a look in. In numbers alone the domestics are the key section in any hospital. If their own lead them, they fight.

Problems of activists

A lot's been written and said about the difficulties women experience rising within the unions. They face direct sexism in prejudice against women leaders. They face indirect sexism in the difficulty of getting to meetings outside working time. But workplace trade unionism is still the easiest place for a working woman to grow and feel her power.

Many women have to go home when they clock off and look after the kids. Most women without children at home are still expected to have the man's dinner on the table and talk to him. Political activity puts a lot of strain on any relationship.

Nobody in their right mind wants their partner going to meetings every night of the week. You get lonely if that happens. This is equally true for both men and women. There's only so much television you can watch by yourself. He grows away from you. He starts to talk about things you don't understand that would bore you if you did understand. His friends are no longer your friends. It's likely he'll start sleeping with somebody else and then let you know how much more interesting and progressive she is than you. When you complain about the empty nights he tells you it's his duty to go to meetings. You know it's ego and ambition. Worse, you know it's more fun plotting down at the pub than watching television with you.

Nobody likes seeing their loved one turn into a mad activist. Women react with the defences of the weak. They bitch, they nag, they sulk. Men react with the defences of the strong. They put their feet down. They forbid.

This is one of the main reason certain sorts of political organisations are dominated by men: the National Union of Teachers, for instance, the trades councils or most left parties. Influence in these organisations depends on going to branch meetings, the executive meetings, the meetings to plot about what to say at the executive meetings, the evening pickets and the Saturday demonstrations and the caucus before the regional quarterlies. The people who can manage these endless meetings are usually men. There is also a leavening of single women and a few women whose partners are activists too. Both men and women tend to be white-collar workers. Many manual workers are exhausted by the time they get home from work.

With workplace politics, it's different, and almost all hospital unionism is workplace politics. Meetings are held in work time or not at all. Women manual workers can be active without ruining their marriages or collapsing physically. There is often strain at home. The husband is frightened by the changes taking place in his wife. Many women activists have an unspoken agreement that they leave the union behind them at work. They make sure they get straight home from work to do the cooking and cleaning. This leaves them tired. But they've always been tired.

Hospital unions are also easier for women to organise in because they're based on women. Most women hospital workers are in jobs that are all, or mostly, done by women. It may take 'positive discrimination' to get a woman MP. The cleaners' steward just about *has* to be a woman. And most of her political life is spent talking to the women she works with. When it comes to negotiations and full-timers she's in a man's world. Most of her life is spent in a woman's world. Her training and growth there can give her the confidence to move upwards and outwards in the union.

Of course, none of this means that women now dominate the hospital unions. Nowhere are they represented in proportion to their number in the workforce. They are especially rare at the level of full-timers and national executives. This may affect the careers of individual women. But full-timers and executives seem to behave much the same no matter who they are. It's at the steward and branch secretary level that the union lives or dies. Here, things are changing. They're not good. But they're better than they were, and a lot better than they are elsewhere. This has strengthened the hospital unions enormously.

3. Struggles

In the last chapter we looked at the unions in terms of the day-to-day life of stewards and union officials. We saw persistence and dedication, but also weakness, disunity and routine. In this chapter we turn to the history of struggle in the last ten years. Here we begin to see the strength of the unions: the workers themselves. In the previous chapter we saw how many women have changed during their participation in the fights against pay policy and the cuts. In this chapter we will look in detail at how both men and women changed and learned during these battles.

Pay policy

For perhaps twenty years every government has been deeply concerned with holding down workers' wages. When they felt strong, they moved in with an official pay policy. When they felt weak, they tried to bargain group by group. In either case, the hospital workers bore the brunt.

They are the largest group of manual workers with whom the government negotiates directly. The government has to prove the seriousness of its intentions by taking on the hospital workers. In private industry, there was 'wage drift', piecework, and the possibility of large settlements in the years between official pay policies. In the hospitals none of this was possible.

Also, the government usually felt the hospital workers were a soft touch. They took note of some of the weaknesses I have set out. And they usually calculated that there would be little public sympathy for a strike. Each year the government offers hospital workers a bit less than local authority workers or teachers, not to mention miners and railway workers.

The government and union leaders, though, have regularly been forced into confrontations that neither side wanted. The first of these was in 1972–73. Historically, the early 1970s marked a high tide of militancy in the British working class. Feeling spread far beyond traditional sections like the miners. It included whole groups who had never been on strike before, like the post office and the hospital workers. And the rubbish collectors, who won a partial victory over pay limits. Their pay deal was traditionally linked to the hospital manual workers'. The council manuals settled on 1 November each year and the hospital ancillaries on 1 December. The ancillary rate was always close to what the council manuals had already won.

The rubbish collectors thus set an example for the hospital ancillaries. Not that the hospital union leaders actually called a national strike. Rather, it began with a spontaneous walkout in Bristol. A wave of partial strikes swept through British hospitals: sectional action here, a three-day strike there, a one-week strike another place. The union leaders scrabbled to support the strikes and signed a deal as fast as they could. It was a reasonable deal.

The strike in itself was no great victory. But it changed the way workers *felt*. Hospital workers had thought their industry would never strike. Now they had been on strike for the first time in their lives. Militants discovered themselves on picket lines up and down the country. At the end of the strike they went back into the hospitals and got themselves elected stewards. They took up one case after another. If the head porter had previously dished out overtime in return for drinks in the pub, he was now held to a proper rota. The cleaner who hadn't had a new mop in three years got one. The porters got a fridge in their rest room. Now nobody could be fired out of hand because their face didn't fit. Management had been unnerved by the strike. They didn't really know where they were or what the workers were capable of. Confident stewards righted wrongs and in the process built up a union organisation and created more stewards.

Other sections watched the ancillaries with interest. The ambulance drivers came out on a series of strikes over pay. The nurses were disdainful of striking, but came out on demonstra-

tions in 1974. They won themselves massive rises in the sub-
sequent Halsbury report. Radiographers stubbornly campaigned
for regrading. Junior hospital doctors threatened to work to rule.

Cuts

Then in 1974 the Labour government was elected. Within
eighteen months a programme of cuts began in the NHS. The
immediate occasion for these cuts was a sterling crisis and an IMF
loan. The IMF demanded 'cuts in public expenditure'. But hospitals were being closed *before* the sterling crisis. The cuts were
part of the long-term strategy of British capital. And not just
British capital. Every national ruling class faces declining profits
and a sick world economy. Each has to cut costs. Cuts unload
some of the social costs onto the working class. As a bonus, they
serve to demoralise and cripple the union movement.

Hospitals are an area capital has to watch particularly carefully.
Left to itself, health expenditure climbs inexorably.

It's a labour-intensive industry, which means it's hard to find
increases in productivity. Scientific progress tends to open up
more possible operations and keep people alive for longer. So
the 'demand' for medicine grows. In the United States, for
instance, expenditure on health is already about 10 per cent of
the Gross National Product (GNP). In Britain it's only about 5
per cent of a much smaller GNP. This is partly because Britain
has the NHS. The government can hold down doctors' earnings
and ration the supply of medicine directly. But in Britain, too,
expenditure on health has been rising for some time.

Hospital expenditure has traditionally been under the formal
control of boards of governors. These boards were left over from
the days when hospitals were either private or municipal charities.
Each board covered a hospital or a group of hospitals. Many
were rank Tories, but they saw their job as helping the hospitals.
And they naturally deferred to the prestige and experience of the
senior doctors: the consultants.

So did hospital management. A typical hospital manager would
be a retired army officer with a moustache. At forty he found
himself with a pension and a training in organisation and disci-

pline. He wanted now to do something useful and gentle. His job was largely making sure the building ran smoothly, overseeing squabbles among ancillary management, and attending sherry parties. On a day-to-day basis he left the consultants to run the hospital. They made the thousands of little decisions about services which added up to an 'expenditure drift'. Whatever you may think of the consultants, they were genuinely concerned with the patients' health.

The power of the consultants had to be broken if hospital spending was to be limited. The government set about this in the early 1970s (Enoch Powell was Minister of Health). The old semi-autonomous boards of governors were replaced by district managements. These were responsible to area managements. Areas reported to region and region to the DHSS in Whitehall. These new structures went with a new breed of managers. They were supposed to run the service on a cost-effective basis and bring the consultants into line. The model for all this was industry, with its independent factories closely supervised by the accountants at head office.

These changes couldn't all be pushed through at one go. The old managers were mostly still in place and the consultants were stubborn foes. But, bit by bit, the style of management changed. This had serious consequences for the unions. Stewards had been accustomed to dealing with benevolent paternalists, who'd demanded politeness and didn't much like unions. But the paternalists were often prepared to right gross wrongs. The unions got into the habit of arguing a case on its merits. They also got into the habit of threatening partial actions. These would outrage the consultants by making their work impossible. Then the consultants would force the management to give in. Now the unions faced managers who saw themselves as politicians, not judges. The lack of hypocrisy was refreshing. But the determination to break the unions was frightening. And threatening partial actions carried less clout now that the consultants were so much weaker.

These changes in management prepared the ground for the cuts. The cuts themselves took four forms: cutting supplies, closing small hospitals, cutting departments in big hospitals, and changing rosters and overtime levels. The first cuts were usually in supplies. Orders took much longer to come through, and management sent around circulars asking everybody to use the backs of old circulars for their memos. These new circulars were not printed on recycled paper. These cuts were frustrating. You never seemed to get what you needed to do the job properly. But they didn't save much money. After all, the main cost in the industry was wages.

Hospital closures

Closing small hospitals presented attractive 'savings'. The hospitals had grown up all higgledy-piggledy. One area had a maternity hospital founded by the Salvation Army. Another had an old workhouse now used as a dumping ground for geriatrics. A third had a large psychiatric hospital because it was located in attractive and soothing countryside. When the NHS began in 1948 it simply took over whatever hospitals were around.

These small hospitals were very 'inefficient'. They cost a lot in support services. Both big hospitals and small need a night telephonist, a night cook, a radiographer, a pharmacist, a pathology lab, and so on. It takes as long in many cases to do ten tests as it does to do twenty. It made better economic sense to centralise services by knocking down little hospitals and building big ones.

Only, of course, they didn't build the big new hospitals. So each small hospital closed represented a *loss* of services, not a *saving*. And it turned out that people liked small hospitals. The workers preferred them because they were cosier: more friendly and less hierarchical. The workers in a small hospital had been working together, loving and hating each other, for twenty and thirty years. They had a community, a working home. They didn't want to lose it.

The patients liked small hospitals, too. It was important to have a casualty department nearby in emergencies. It was easier for friends and relatives to visit if they didn't have to take three buses. Many small hospitals were geriatric and chronic long-stay places. Visiting was particularly important for these patients. So was the homier feel of the small hospital.

Workers were outraged by any threat to their hospital. They wanted something done about it. But management weren't stupid. Small hospitals tended to have weak unions. Management usually went for the places where the unions were little more than a shell. And they cut the hospital down, step by step. First they closed the casualty department, so there was no steady supply of patients. Then they closed the stores or the laundry or the kitchen, so the hospital couldn't survive on its own. They employed lots of agency nurses. When the time came for closure they could simply send the agency nurses home. They ran down the hospital generally and kept the wards understaffed. Working conditions got so bad the nurses didn't want to keep the hospital open. They felt it wasn't a fit place for patients. Throughout all this, management denied that they planned to close the place. Then, then it was half-closed and wholly demoralised, they quickly shut it.

Until recently, management was able to promise everybody at least some kind of job in another hospital. Many workers simply went. They were unhappy about it, but they couldn't see how to fight it.

In most hospitals, the workers saw closure coming a long way off. In a few, they had strong union organisation. Take St Matthew's, a small geriatric hospital in East London. There, management moved to close the kitchens and bring in food from a central kitchen. The ancillaries all walked out, and immediately tried to spread the strike. Within three days, the management had given in completely. They even paid the workers for the days they were on strike. Six years later St Matthew's is still there.

Of course, lots of small hospitals around St Matthew's have since closed. Management's strategy over the cuts has been to feel out each group of workers. They retreated where it looked like too much trouble and went elsewhere for their cuts.

St Matthew's had two very good and very confident stewards when the threat of closure hit. Few other small hospitals were as lucky or as combative. But many parts of the country saw hospital occupations. In London alone there was Poplar Hospital, the Bethnal Green, Wood Green, St Mary's, St Columba's, the

Elizabeth Garrett Anderson – and more. Many other campaigns against closure were quite active but never managed to get an occupation together. Each occupation was different. But they had certain similarities.

First, much of the initial drive for the occupations came from outside the hospital. Local socialists and stewards from other hospitals decided something had to be done. They walked into the threatened hospital and started talking to the stewards. These stewards were desperate for somebody to talk to. A campaign committee of local militants and the stewards inside the hospital was set up. The stewards were convinced of the need for an occupation, and they convinced the workers. The campaign committee began running around local workplaces and trades councils. They distributed leaflets, handed out petitions and organised demonstrations.

The occupation tactic appealed to both campaign committee and stewards. The campaign committee liked it because it was so left-wing: it reminded them of articles they'd read about the Italian working class. It wasn't just your boring 'economistic' English strike. It posed the alternative political economy of workers' control. It would open up people's consciousness. And it was a way the militants could participate actively. They also had more experience of campaigns than of strikes.

The stewards liked the idea of an occupation because they loved their hospital and thought the cuts were obscene. But they didn't have the confidence in themselves to lead a strike. And they didn't think their members would strike. After all, they never had before. Until those militants walked into the hospital, they'd been at their wits' end. They didn't really trust all those people from the SWP, and the like. They knew perfectly well that the left is out to mislead and manipulate workers. But they liked them personally and they needed all the friends they could get. And an occupation looked like a possible way to fight.

But there were problems. It wasn't at all clear exactly what an occupation involved. In most cases, it meant a work-in, but one with management still in charge. There was none of the excitement and feeling of a world turned upside down that you can get in a factory occupation. Cleaners were still cleaners and nurses still nurses. The head porter was still hauling people up to the office on disciplinaries. The occupation didn't really touch many workers in their daily lives.

Another problem was keeping a supply of patients coming in and the doctors to treat them. Local GPs had to be written to and visited and persuaded to keep referring patients. The casualty doctor had to be persuaded to put his career on the line by refusing a transfer. The campaign had to be acceptable to the consultants. In fact, it needed their active support.

This meant there was an awful lot you couldn't do. Individual doctors did feel strongly enough to risk their careers. Consultants did feel outraged by the cuts and threatened by a loss of position. But they were moderate and careful men. They would support work-ins in these extraordinary circumstances. But they didn't trust the campaign committee. They didn't want the unions running the campaign inside the hospital. They wanted a committee of all staff, dominated by professionals. And they didn't want to hear any talk of strikes.

A third problem was simple exhaustion. Management weren't stupid or precipitate. They kept postponing any final decision on the hospital. There was an appeal; or the area health authority was thinking it over; or the minister was considering the matter. The occupation would last for months and sometimes years. The bulk of the work fell on a few people on the committee. The active stewards would spend their days trying to hold the hospital together. Evenings, they ran around to union meetings and tenants' associations and trades councils. They got physically exhausted and emotionally worn out. Their partners began to suspect they were sleeping with somebody else.

The root cause of this exhaustion was that the occupation didn't involve the majority of the workers. In a strike, it's easy to find people to visit other workplaces. They are excited by the strike, they are desperate to win, and they have the time. But the occupations were different. The workers felt the committee or their stewards could do all that.

With time, the occupations began to wear thin. The workers got tired of all the uncertainty. A few people accepted transfers, and weren't replaced. The hospital ran down and the supply of patients slowly dried up. After months or years, management made their move.

At that point, a strike was the only answer. There were strikes in support of most occupied hospitals. Workers from other hospitals and other industries joined in. But these were one-day strikes. They encouraged the occupied hospital, but they couldn't be repeated. An all-out strike was needed to win. It didn't happen.

In London, the crunch came over the Hounslow Hospital. This small hospital in West London was occupied for months and months. Finally, management came in with strong police protection. They pushed past the lone picket at the front. They forced sick and confused patients into taxis and bundled them off to other hospitals. The staff on the wards didn't fight back. Partly they were astonished and partly they didn't want to upset confused elderly patients with hand-to-hand fighting. But mostly it was that nothing in their nursing lives had prepared them for room-to-room fighting with a superior force of policemen. They stood and cried. Management set to work with axes to break up the beds and wreck the wards so the hospital couldn't be used again.

Next day, all the papers and the TV news carried pictures of the vandalised wards. If ever there was going to be a strike over the cuts in London, this was it. Representatives of about fifteen hospitals met in a hurried evening meeting and called an all-out strike. Mass meetings at twelve hospitals voted to strike the next day. But only the West London Hospital voted for an all-out strike. The rest went for a one-day protest. There was an angry march to the area health authority meeting that day. Geoffrey Drain of NALGO was booed off the platform for refusing to make the strike official. It was over. The battle was lost.

All over London, militants realised that occupations were useless without strike backing. At the next NUPE conference there was an attempt to call for an official strike in support of another occupied hospital: London's Elizabeth Garrett Anderson. The NUPE leadership refused to let it be discussed at the conference. The writing was on the wall.

Which didn't mean there were no more hospital occupations.

There were several. For the occupations had by no means been complete failures. After all, they largely took place in hospitals where the stewards didn't expect their members to strike anyway. The eventual closure came months or years after it would have happened otherwise. Thousands of sick people got treatment they would have missed otherwise.

And it wasn't the fault of the workers at the Hounslow that they couldn't get other workers out in support for more than a day. The occupations weren't a failure or a waste of time. But they were a defeat.

The danger in these defeats was the taste left in the mouths of the hospital workers involved. By and large, the lesson they learned was that militant union action didn't work; you couldn't win. The occupation tactic had not been presented to them for what it was: a desperate strategem born of weakness. It was mostly presented as the highest possible form of struggle. And if that didn't work, what would?

Staffing levels

It's hard to prove it, but the occupations must have made management hesitate before closing many small hospitals. In any case they couldn't make enough savings by closing small hospitals alone. They had to go for the staffing levels in the big places as well.

Management's first tactic here was the bonus scheme. The union leaders were enthusiastic about bonus schemes in the wake of the 1973 strike, particularly in NUPE. Here were all these low-paid workers. It was hard to win much for them on the national level. But on a local level management was offering increases of one-fifth or one-third on basic rates. Many workers leapt at the chance.

Wondrous to declare, there was a catch. NHS management is bound by an iron law that all bonus schemes must be 'self-financing'. This means that the workers in a section can get a higher rate, but their total wage bill must not rise. Indeed, it must fall. That's the whole point of a bonus scheme from management's point of view.

There are only two ways the total bill can fall. One is through job wastage. Four men receive the wages of five for doing the work of six. They benefit as individuals and management benefits collectively. It's easy to scorn people for signing such deals. Yet in the last fifteen years most sections of workers in Britain have signed similar productivity deals. Low-paid hospital workers say they have to do it to survive. The alternative is usually the cuts without the bonus.

The other way to reduce total earnings is to fool around with rosters and overtime. This is a complicated business. I once spent a quiet evening on a picket line with two senior stewards. They were leading a group of porters on a long strike over new rosters. They spent an hour trying to explain to me in detail what the effect of the new rosters would be. They showed me charts and examples. I'd been a portering steward myself and thought I knew the book backwards. After an hour, they gave up trying to make me understand. Kindly, they said not to worry – the blokes on strike didn't understand the details either. And there was only one man on the management side who seemed to grasp the arithmetic.

But to simplify a bit, let's start with rest-day and off-day working. Many hospital workers do a basic five-day week. An example would be Monday, Wednesday, Thursday, Friday and Sunday. Tuesday is their 'rest day' and Saturday is their 'off day'. They are paid double-time if they work the 'rest day', and time-and-a-half if they work the 'off day'. They have one day's regular overtime as well. If they work it on their rest day they get paid double-time. If they work it on their off day they get time-and-a-half. For years, their regular rota has had them working on the Tuesday, the 'rest day'. They have been paid the basic rate for Monday, Wednesday, Thursday and Friday. They've got double time for Tuesday and Saturday. That's eight days' pay for six days' work. Now management wants them to come in on their off day: Saturday, instead of the Tuesday. They will only get time-and-a-half, or seven-and-a-half days' pay in total. That's a 6 per cent pay cut. (Trust me on that bit of arithmetic.) Also, it means they have to work every weekend for the rest of their time in this job. This won't please their families.

Another thing management can do is simply cut out overtime altogether. Then they're down to six days' pay, a 25 per cent pay cut. Or management can try to set worker against worker by cutting some people's Tuesdays and leaving other people their Wednesdays.

In the early 1970s the first wave of bonus schemes tended to concentrate on job losses. It didn't seem so bad to agree to job losses then, and there was sufficient slack so there were no compulsory redundancies. Since the late 1970s the newer bonus schemes have gone for overtime cuts and roster changes as well.

Almost every section of hospital workers in most hospitals has experienced these cuts in staffing and take-home wages. In the weakly organised sections, management simply announced new rotas. Or they quietly failed to replace workers who left, and redistributed the work among those remaining. Management bought out the stronger sections with bonus schemes. Once those sections had got used to bonus schemes, management returned a few years later with a new, and worse, bonus scheme.

Of course, the unions often fought these schemes. The stewards spent months haggling over details. They called in the branch secretary and the full-timer. They queried this and objected to that. But in the end it came down to striking or accepting the deal. And even winning a strike only kept the wolf from the door for a while.

Take, for example, the porters at St Francis's Hospital. In 1976, they faced the first cuts. Management closed two wards. They wanted to reorganise the catering rosters and get the porters to take on extra duties. The enraged porters decided not to cover for vacant posts. The filing clerk on nights had left and hadn't been replaced. The night manager ordered three porters to get some files. One by one, they each refused and were sacked. One of them was the NUPE branch secretary. By morning, all the ancillaries were out on strike. In three days, management buckled and reinstated the men.

But at the same time the cuts in catering did go through. Over the next few years the domestics, the worst-organised section, put up with cut after cut. After a couple of years, the porters felt they had to accept a new bonus deal. This preserved the hours and rosters of all men currently employed. But all new men started on worse rosters. By 1982, there were only six porters out of thirty left on the old rosters. Then management tried to rewrite the rosters again. The porters came out on strike for eight weeks. They were largely on their own. Catering and the cleaners had already been demoralised by the cuts, though catering did come out with them for a week. The other hospitals in the district had had their union organisation cut to pieces in the last six years. At the end of eight weeks the porters agreed to a compromise. The terms were complex. Basically it left them worse off than before, but much better off than they would have been on the rosters first proposed.

The porters at St Francis's were relatively well organised. They had among their ranks the branch secretary, the branch chair and two stewards. They had been out on strike over pay with other hospital workers in 1973 and 1979. They had joined in several one-day strikes over the cuts. Their work as shift porters brought them together in the long night hours. There were a lot of strong personal friendships between them. Their strike was determined: they knew it would be a long one when they started. Their strike meetings were a model of effective democracy. Every porter spoke his thoughts and fears honestly and nobody jeered. They fought far harder than any group of hospital workers around, and they did much better. But the cuts chipped away at them, too.

The insidious thing about the cuts was that management could keep coming back for another bite of the cherry. You couldn't keep going on strike. Even if you won, you still lost the money for the time you were out. When you went back you seemed no better off than before. It was a defensive war, and one by one the workers' positions were worn away.

What's more, they were worn away because, at some crucial point, somebody didn't stand by them. Maybe the laundry lost hours and the porters sat by and let it happen. When the porters were threatened they went to the laundry for help – and none was forthcoming. Then the canteen was in trouble and there was no strong section left for them to turn to.

Cuts divided people. Management took on the workers section

by section and hospital by hospital. Workers usually didn't feel confident enough for a general fight, so they almost automatically began to argue why *they* shouldn't get the chop. At one hospital, people argued that it should be kept open because it was a women's hospital. At another, it was because it was a children's hospital. At a third, the workers said it should be kept open because it was in East London and the East Enders had nothing. On a more personal level, the first whiff of redundancies made people start looking around to see exactly who would go: me, you or her?

Cuts campaigns

Local actions fragmented the working class. Most hospital workers saw from early on that the problem had to be tackled on a wider basis. The national unions came under intense pressure from the activists to do something on a national level.

What they did was to mount campaigns and call one-day strikes. NUPE led the way in this. The union had been built up in the 1930s by campaigns and demonstrations which brought pressure to bear on local councillors. In 1973, the unions had mounted a low-pay campaign. What could be more natural than a cuts campaign?

There were stickers, posters, buttons by the tens of thousands. The graphics were first rate, the leaflets among the best ever produced in Britain. There were motions at the TUC and Labour Party conferences. Stern, uncompromising motions. There were one-day strikes over the cuts.

In London, the first of these was called by the London division of NUPE, in October 1976. It was massive, with 80,000 demonstrators; many more people stayed away from work. The union leaders were astonished. But of course, the workers in individual hospitals were already living the cuts. They were galvanised by the idea of some all-London action. A national demonstration and one-day strike in the spring was equally successful. After that, what? More one-day strikes and demonstrations.

It was easy for the union activists to bring their members out the first time. It was harder the second time, but we did it. The third time, it was very difficult. The workers at the union meeting asked awkward questions. 'What did the last two strikes achieve except lose us money? What is the third going to achieve?' The workers said one-day strikes didn't work. The stewards couldn't think what to say. And on the day, that hospital stayed in.

Then we saw the real beauty of the one-day strike as a tactic. Now the leadership of the union turned round and said there was nothing they could do. The members weren't prepared to fight. The leadership had responded to pressure from below to *do something*. They couldn't be accused of not being militant or of selling out. But somehow the result was the same as it would have been if they had sold out.

This was particularly clear when there was a possibility of serious action. In East London in 1977 several hospitals faced closure. The left was very strong in the stewards' committees. At the crucial meeting of the area stewards, the SWP argued for an all-out East London strike to keep the hospitals open. The NUPE and ASTMS full-timers argued for one-day stoppages and a campaign of lightning strikes. The full-timers won. The one-day strike went ahead very successfully. The hospitals closed.

In West London, the strike over the closure of Hounslow Hospital had to be reorganised unofficially. None of the unions was willing to give an official call. And while NUPE supported the Elizabeth Garrett Anderson and the majority union there, the NUPE conference wasn't allowed to discuss an all-out strike in support of the EGA.

Why? Simple treason? Perhaps, in a few cases. But generally, no. What happened was that the union leaders found themselves in a cleft stick. The Labour government was under pressure to attack the working class. The centrepiece of this attack was the cuts. The union leaders had to object to each individual cut. They had to be seen to be fighting the cuts or their unions would fall apart. But to stop *all* the cuts was unthinkable. It would destroy the Labour government and let in the Tories. They would, of course, be worse. Destroying Labour wouldn't make anybody very popular on the TUC General Council. More important, the union leaders couldn't see any real alternative to capitalism or the Labour Party. After all, they weren't revolutionaries. Their members weren't either. They wouldn't have got elected or appointed if they had been revolutionaries. So they couldn't see any alternative to Labour.

The union leadership mounted a campaign to influence the Labour Party. They knew the leaders of the party. They wouldn't necessarily listen to reason, but they would listen to sufficient pressure from the unions. They had backed down over plans for union reform, 'In Place of Strife', in 1969. They would back down again. Demonstrations and speeches would swing the TUC against the cuts. The TUC would move the government. They did, in fact, swing the TUC. But they didn't move the government. The union leaders' tactics were a failure.

For the leaders of the Labour Party hadn't been kidding. The economy was in crisis. They didn't have any room to manoeuvre within capitalism. They had to cut. And cut they did. The union leaders couldn't understand it. They went on howling about every cut and retreating every time a real fight loomed up. The one-day strikes allowed them to get away with this. They could do something with failure guaranteed.

Cuts and consciousness

The cuts led to disunity, anger and demoralisation. But, in contradictory ways, they also strengthened the unions. All sorts of people started joining unions because their jobs were in danger. In many hospitals the unions had always ignored the part-time evening cleaners and the evening cleaners had ignored the union. Now, the union stewards went looking for the evening cleaners because they wanted support for a one-day strike. The evening cleaners went looking for the stewards to do something about the cuts. Much the same thing happened with night nurses and clerical staff. As a result, the unions kept growing even as jobs were disappearing.

The cuts also produced a slow sea-change in people's attitudes. There were no more soft options or quiet jobs. Everybody's job got harder. A lot of people were yelling at you for not doing things you simply didn't have time for. The pressure built up.

Nurses found the cuts particularly galling. In the end, it was the nurses who had to deliver the cuts to the sick. If the laundry was short staffed and didn't do the patients' clothes, the nurses watched the patients sit in last night's pyjamas all day. If the canteen and the food budget were cut, the nurses had to feed fattening stodge to the patients. If the porters couldn't bring the drugs, it was the nurses who tore their hair out. They were busier and busier making tea and mopping floors and doing the other things the domestics who used to be there used to do. The more they had to do that and the more short staffed they were, the less proper caring they could do themselves. The job became more of a burden and less of a vocation.

Ambulance drivers, too, saw the cutting edge of government policy. Again and again, they would pick up a case and realise the local casualty department was closed. So they got on the radio and asked control where to take the patient. Control called round the hospitals madly to find a spare bed. The ambulance drove round in circles for fifteen minutes or half-an-hour. Very occasionally, the patient died. Almost always the patient lived. But ambulance drivers got a clear view of the cuts.

This sort of thing undermined the moral argument against striking. Both ambulance drivers and nurses had always been told they shouldn't strike because it would put the patients at risk. Many believed this. But now such arguments were hypocrisy when management itself was reducing the service permanently to a level which almost no strikes achieved even temporarily.

It wasn't just nurses and ambulance drivers who noticed what was going on. Everybody did. When hospital workers went on strike, they still felt guilty when the papers attacked them. But if the newspaper quoted one of their administrators they stopped feeling guilty. 'The nerve of him, after what he's done.'

The winter of discontent

The legacy of the cuts campaigns was bitterness and demoralisation. The bitterness found its expression in the 'winter of discontent', the 1978–79 national campaign over low pay. As in 1973, this was a battle the union leaders had been forced into.

They had signed the 'social contract' and delivered three years of wage control. They had enough links with the rank and file to know they couldn't deliver a fourth year. They told Callaghan so, and urged him to take his Labour government into an autumn election in 1978. He gave a speech at the TUC that seemed to promise such an election. The union leaders breathed a sigh of relief. Then Callaghan put off the election. He didn't believe the TUC, and he wanted another year in historic 10 Downing Street.

Wage restraint cracked almost immediately. The Ford workers went out in the autumn and very publicly smashed the 5 per cent limit. Other groups soon followed them. In the private sector the government's 5 per cent policy was in ribbons. But in the public sector there was no backing down to their own employees. Here, they held the line at 5 per cent.

Neither council workers nor ancillaries were that keen to go on strike. In September 1978, experienced stewards laughed at the idea that there would be any fight over wages that winter. But public employees had been stuck with the letter of the last three pay policies. Many hospital ancillaries had seen their pay fall drastically through loss of overtime. They were bitter over the cuts. And they weren't willing to settle for a lower deal than other workers just to save the Labour government's face. So the union leaders didn't dare to sign on the government's terms.

Nor, of course, did they dare to lead an all-out strike. The word from the leadership was to sound out your members. Bring out anybody who is prepared to do anything. Once again, we had sectional strikes, working to rule, overtime bans and one-day strikes here and there.

As before, this was a hell of a way to run a strike. The strong sections complained that they always had to fight for everybody else. The weaker sections were confirmed in their weakness. They went into work while other people did their fighting for them. And most of those who went into work were women and most of those who took strike action were men. Which only confirmed the idea that women workers were weak and passive.

Sectional actions usually took the form of working to rule or banning overtime. Working to rule was often difficult for people like porters who didn't work together and could be isolated by management anywhere in a large building and bullied into doing something. It also increased friction between the section working to rule and other staff. And there are problems with overtime bans, too. Usually there's one scab in every section who'll take every hour of overtime that's going. The workers can't see the overtime ban having much effect. Since it's a sectional action, they can see that the transport and the porters aren't losing anything. And every week Fred the scab waves his pay slip in their faces. The management goes around saying that if you leave the union you can have all the overtime you want. After five or six weeks a couple of blokes take the overtime. Then the steward quickly calls off the overtime ban before the union crumbles.

It was a weak, half-hearted campaign. It was also largely successful. The government did eventually bow to pressure and set up the Clegg Commission to inquire into low pay. Clegg's eventual report did lead to increases substantially more than 5 per cent. By any normal standards, the 'winter of discontent' was a victory for the unions.

But on the wards and in the mess rooms it often felt like a defeat. Partly, there was no obvious initial victory because Clegg took months to report. Partly, the actions had been sectional. Those who did take action usually experienced a gradual erosion of their strength. Those who didn't take action didn't experience a victory. And of course the full claim was nowhere near won.

Yet the feeling of defeat also came from the emotions behind the discontent. The dispute was over wages. But the talk on the picket lines was of cuts. The energy that had been diffused and broken in local fights was concentrated on the national pay battle. In a capitalist society, unions and workers usually can't see how to challenge capitalism as a whole: that's what stopping the cuts would have meant. But they can see how to fight over wages. The fight over cuts is an unending defensive battle. The fight over wages is short, sharp and winnable. You can get 12 per cent instead of 5.

We live in a materialist society. In our lives the lack of money comes to stand for our lack of happiness. Hating our jobs, we go out at the lunch hour and buy some expensive 'treat'. Just so did the wages issue channel all the hospital workers' anger. Yet when they won on wages they also realised they hadn't won on cuts. Management could claw back any increases by firing staff and rewriting rosters.

In a way, it was like the 1980 national steel strike. On any rational criteria the steel workers won that dispute. But since they were out over money alone they went back with no possibility of halting the destruction of their industry. In both cases, what in the 1960s would have been a big working-class victory was now lived through as a defeat.

The union leaders had their own reasons for regretting their victory. Looking back, they saw it as the reason the Tories won the election. After all, the media and bitter Labour politicians told them NUPE in particular had lost Labour the election. Union leaders were embarrassed. The widespread press campaign scared them, too. That year 1979 was the heyday of Fleet Street's picket: a callous greedy lumpen picket, who closed down the kids' hospital and chuckled over the threat of cholera in the streets. The union leaders were held up to the public as the instigators of all this. They were ashamed of the image they and their members presented to the public. They determined that never again would they lose 'public sympathy'.

The way to gain public sympathy if you're on strike isn't to gain a good press. You might as well hope for Margaret Thatcher to be visited by the ghost of Christmas Past. The way is to get out to other groups of workers and tell them what it's all about. But this isn't the way trade union leaders work. They issue press releases. And if the press tells them the public is against them, they panic.

Partly as a consequence, the leaders agreed to change the date of the ancillary settlement. Traditionally, the hospital ancillaries had settled a month after the council manuals. Their pay deals were inevitably linked. We have seen what that led to in 1973 and 1979. The government had no intention of facing the same alliance again. They wanted to move the settlement date to 1 April. That would coincide with the settlements of docile hospital workers, like the nurses and clericals. In the hope of avoiding another bad winter, the union leaders agreed. The consequence was that three years later they had the biggest wave of strikes the hospitals had ever seen.

Those strikes were different in composition and impact from anything that had gone before: in 1982, many nurses came out. Why? Partly, it was because their views had been changed by the cuts – as I've pointed out, it was the nurses who had to deliver these direct to the patient. But something else was changing their traditional placidity: feminist ideas.

Feminism and nurses

Feminism has affected most ancillary stewards indirectly. It has affected many nurses directly. For many reasons British feminism has been largely contained within the middle class. But nurses see themselves as middle class. Many are very open to feminist ideas. For instance, they use the word 'sexist' in daily conversation. Partly because of feminist ideas, they have begun to see their jobs differently.

The traditional idea of a woman's role has always strongly influenced the traditional idea of a nurse's role. In a phrase, nurses are 'good girls'. The general feeling is still amazingly common among nurses. But it's crumbling. And as nurses stop trying to be 'good girls' they also begin to see themselves as workers.

Sex is often the flashpoint for disputes about nursing and femininity. Traditionally, nurses' homes were closely guarded citadels. There were rigorous rules against male visiting. To this day, many nursing managers feel free to walk into a nurse's room without knocking. They also feel free to tell nurses when they are consorting with unsuitable men. And there are a host of rules about dress.

These days, nurses seem to sleep with pretty much whom they want to, when they want to. Some of the popular myths about their sexual behaviour are pure fantasy. Yet if you stop thinking of yourself as Florence Nightingale you can begin to have good sex. It helps you feel like a woman and it's a good antidote to dealing with the sick and dying. But there's often hell to pay.

In an earlier chapter, I talked about how unions had been built among nurses over the issue of coloured tights. In one way, that's not a serious issue like rosters or winding time. In another way, something deadly serious is at stake. The question being fought out is this: What is a woman and to whom does her body belong? Herself, or management? If nursing management lose that fight, they are liable to lose the rest.

As feminism chips away at 'femininity' it also chips away at 'professionalism'. Matron gives you a ridiculous introductory talk about how to behave in the nurses' home. The same woman tells you about strikes. Nurses do not go on strikes because they are dutiful professionals. They care about the patients. Domestics do go on strike. They aren't professionals. They don't care about the patients. And (usually unspoken, but clearly in the air) *such people can't be expected to care*.

This line is deeply offensive to domestics. It's also untrue. Any nurse who looks carefully can see that Sue who cleans her ward goes out on one-day strikes. She can also see that the same Sue remembers to sneak tobacco in for old Mr Remington. And she knows Sue is the closest confidante of Fred, the pleurisy case in the end bed. She may ignore what she can see. But if she hears the line about strikes from somebody she already knows talks rubbish about sexuality and professionalism, she starts to think. Then she notices that the people who say you mustn't endanger the patients are the same people who have you up in the office for going on a demonstration against the hospital closing. One day she's going to ask herself why not go on strike? Particularly if she's getting pretty fed up with the whole idea of women as combination martyr–doormats.

Conclusion

Such then have been the changes among hospital workers in the last decade. It's important to bear in mind that these changes have been partial. They don't all lead in one direction. By no means all nurses are feminists. Many feminist hospital workers regularly cross picket lines. There may be more women stewards. They may be less dependent on men. But the British working class as a whole is taking a hammering. The stewards are less confident of the strength of their women members than they were five years ago. The fight against the cuts may have brought many people to the point of outrage and some to militancy. But the defeats of the cuts campaigns have led to demoralisation and helplessness. The wages struggles in 1973 and 1979 were more or less successful. But that didn't mean hospital workers have high pay or that ancillaries were anxious for a repeat performance. The cuts struggles may have created many stewards. The threat of the sack has recently held many people back. Common struggles may have united a divided workforce. Defeats and the frictions of daily life have divided them again.

There are many factors at work here. They pull in different directions. Things differ widely from one hospital to another. But hospital workers have all had to react to forces and powers outside their control. In their reactions they have begun to change themselves. The process continued in the pay campaign of 1982. That's the subject of the next chapter.

4. The battle of 1982

The 1982 pay dispute wasn't engineered by the TUC. It was thrust upon them by the government and by their members. Now all hospital workers had the same settlement date for their national pay awards: 1 April. We have seen that this was the result of a government tactic to split the hospital ancillaries off from the council manual workers. But in 1982 it wasn't the council workers who were feeling militant. It was the nurses. The hospital ancillaries had just come through the 'winter of discontent'. Few wished to repeat the experience immediately. The nurses, by contrast, had taken no action since 1974. That year they had won up to 50 per cent increases by demonstrations alone. Many nurses thought of the strike weapon as some sort of bolt from the skies. Because it seemed to them such an extreme step, they thought it would have extreme consequences. The ancillaries weren't so sure.

In the period before the pay negotiations there was little feeling among ancillaries. There was almost no propaganda by the unions or the left. But the nurses read a flood of propaganda from other sources. The Royal College of Nursing mounted a campaign of stickers, posters and demonstrations. They reminded the government that Mrs Thatcher had promised a special deal for the nurses. The nursing press ran large features on how miserable nurses' pay was. Something ought to be done about it, they said. It wasn't exactly clear what. But all over the wards stickers began to appear saying 'nurses deserve a living wage'. It all created a feeling that something would be done.

Then came the offer. It was a straight 6 per cent for nurses and 4 per cent for ancillaries. The government hoped to split the nurses off. Only the nurses showed any sign of activity. The RCN might accept any deal, no matter how bad, as long as it offered them more than other ranks.

But the offer was just too low. The cost of living had gone up 12 per cent in the last year. Most other workers got more: many private sector workers, miners, gas workers, council workers, judges and the police. Civil servants and hospital workers got the bottom offers.

The civil servants had just a long-drawn-out dispute the year before. They weren't likely to offer any resistance. The government thought the hospitals wouldn't fight either. But they weren't unhappy about taking on the hospital workers. The government figured they were badly organised and badly led. They figured the TUC would huff and puff – and call one-day strikes. Nothing they couldn't handle. They also counted on public support in any confrontation with the hospitals. After all, most of the people they knew and all the papers had strongly disapproved of the 'winter of discontent'.

The union leaders didn't know what to do. The nurses expected more. It was impossible just to swallow the offer. So the TUC set up an alliance of all their hospital unions. This alliance called mass meetings of all unions in every hospital. These mass meetings were to consider the offer and what to do about it.

At my hospital, we usually had thirty people for NUPE meetings. Now we had a hundred from every section of the hospital. There were twenty nurses and even one doctor. This alone gave us a feeling of unity and greater strength than we'd ever had before. We disposed of the offer easily. No. Then we got stuck on what action to take. Some people talked of demonstrations or picket lines, some talked of one-day strikes. One porter proposed bringing down the government. He got into an argument with the other porters over the Falklands. One of the cleaners said the nurses would never strike. A nurse yelled 'Why not?' A male nurse shouted 'Dedication doesn't pay my rent.' The feeling was chaotically good. In the end we agreed to take whatever action the TUC advised.

This was the general pattern. NUPE said something like 99 per cent of its branches rejected the offer. But it wasn't very clear to anybody what rejection meant. It was almost a decision without responsibility. There was a long tradition in NUPE of rejecting all offers at mass meetings and then waiting for the leadership to accept them. In the miners' union a rejection of the employer's final offer is also a decision for a national strike. That's why the miners have only rejected the offer four times in this century, and each time they've meant it. By contrast, nobody was certain whether to take the hospitals seriously.

But the TUC leaders clearly had to do something. They followed form and called a one-day strike. It was a rousing success. At our hospital, NUPE and COHSE voted to come out, NALGO to stay in. On the day, the stewards turned up on the picket line not knowing what to expect. A few nurses had said at meetings that they would strike. The stewards weren't sure if they'd actually deliver. By eight, no ancillaries had crossed the picket line. And something like a quarter of the nurses had stayed out, too.

With any other section of workers, that would have been total defeat. For nurses in a London hospital, it was very good. The nurses were buoyant on the picket line. One of them had been on strike once before in another hospital. One had been a shop steward in a factory before becoming a nursing auxiliary. The rest were on strike for the first time in their lives.

It took a lot to get them out the door. The first five nurses to show up announced that they didn't care if they lost their jobs. They were so fed up with the conditions in there – if management wanted to fire them, they fucking well could. They were going to stand on the picket line all day, and nobody was going past them.

We began asking passers-by to sign a petition. To our amazement, everybody did. We got together signs asking anybody who supported us to honk their horns. It was a busy road. Many did. We got ourselves a megaphone and stood out in the middle of the road asking people to honk their horns. It got noisy. The nurses hectored drivers who forgot, using the names on their trucks. 'Hey, Hovis, give us a toot.' A passing driver shouted, 'Go back to work.' Traffic was slow and his car window was open. A nurse leaned in through the window and put the megaphone against his ear and let him have it. 'One of these days you're going to be sick, mate, and you're going to need us. And when you do I'll remember, mate. I'll know your face and you'll die.' The lights changed, and the driver fled.

A policeman came along on the other side of the road. He crossed towards us. The two revolutionaries on the picket line shrank back against the wall, figuring the party was over. One of the nurses walked straight across and met him in the middle of the road. She smiled flirtatiously up into his face from a distance of six inches.

'I'm afraid I have to escort you away from here, constable,' she said, with a friendly laugh. 'If you come across and start to harass those people, I'm going to have to assault you. And we don't want that, do we?'

The policeman didn't really have time to decide if he was going to slug a pretty nurse in uniform in the middle of a busy road. She took him by the arm and led him away down the middle of the road. She shouted at each driver to honk his horn. The policeman waved foolishly at them with his free arm. The police didn't return that day.

The one-day strike was a success. The union leaders found participation all over the country far more solid than they had expected. On the other hand, the one-day strike did nothing to move the government. So the TUC had to find something else to do. In the jargon, they had to 'step up the action'. They decided on more strikes and a campaign to reduce the NHS to accident and emergency cover.

They called two one-day strikes: the first on a Friday and the next on the following Tuesday. This was a masterstroke. It was more militant than a one-day strike. It was twice as much striking. It had exactly the same effect on the government as a one-day strike. (Two times nothing equals nothing.) It lost the members twice as much money. (Two times ten quid is twenty quid.) The TUC was able to step up the action without actually achieving anything other than exhausting the troops.

The TUC also looked round for other weapons. Many hospitals were already threatening the management with sectional strikes unless they reduced admissions. The TUC backed this. The idea was to bring pressure to bear on the government. But of course Thatcher of the Falklands wouldn't mind if the whole NHS closed down. The only thing that worried her was support from other workers.

At first, very few hospital workers could see how to build this support. The few members of the revolutionary left, particularly the SWP, had spent years taking groups of striking workers around workplaces to meet the stewards and ask for support. The people with experience in fighting hospital hospital closures had been round the local workplaces too and knew the stewards. So these few people started organising delegations to local work-places. It was second nature, and in our dreams we hoped for support strikes. In our waking moments we hoped for a collection and a chance to address a union meeting. A hospital worker could get up and be cheered. She'd feel great and that would stiffen the strike.

That's how it worked out at first in our hospital. In Sheffield, it was different. The day of the first strike the local SWP cajoled ten hospital workers into cars, mainly nurses and occupational therapists. They took them on a tour of the local pits. To every-body's amazement, four of those pits were on strike by lunchtime. By the next day, hospital militants all over the country knew it was possible. Of course, the Yorkshire miners were special. Of course, it wasn't simple working-class solidarity: it was partly because it was nurses who'd made the call. But the barrier had been broken. We knew we could get solidarity strikes. With that, we knew we could win. An all-out strike would enable us to send out flying pickets. We could bring out the mines. With the mines and the hospitals out, we could capture the imagination of the working class and walk all over Thatcher. Suddenly, there was mad joy and hope.

So we came out for the two one-day strikes. Not everywhere, certainly. Many places picked one of the days and worked the other. They felt the impact would be the same. But the strikes were solid and the feeling was good. In the middle of these strikes came the union conferences.

It was the first time in history that the NUPE and COHSE leadership had to face a rank-and-file body of any authority during a dispute. Again, nobody knew what would happen. NUPE met first. On the opening day there was an emergency resolution from Sheffield calling for an all-out strike. It was carried overwhelmingly, with just a few abstentions. That evening the militants were drunk with delight.

The NUPE leadership were visibly shaken. They were almost at a loss for words in the TV interviews as they left the conference. By that evening, they had figured out a line. The NUPE conference had voted for an all-out strike, but that didn't mean there was going to be one. This was a joint effort by all the unions and NUPE couldn't strike out on their own. Our great strength this time was that we were acting together. We had no intention of dissipating that. The conference decision meant that NUPE would argue in TUC meetings for an all-out strike. And just as soon as they converted Geoffrey Drain of NALGO to the general strike, we would have one.

It was the old 'NUPE trick' with a vengeance. Every activist felt they had to tie the leadership down. On the second day of the conference, the Stockport delegate stood up. He moved the suspension of standing orders so they could set a date for the strike to begin. Standing orders were suspended. There was quiet. Nobody stood up to name the day.

Why? Because Bill, the delegate, had been on the phone home to Sheila, early in the morning before the session began. Sheila was the branch chair, holding things together back at the hospital. He told her about the exciting decision. Sheila reminded him of some things. 'Bill, I don't think our members are going to do it. They haven't voted for it. We're low paid and we live week to week. They keep saying to me that if they go out for two weeks they'll go under. And how are we going to strike here if COHSE walk across our picket lines? Remember, we got them out last time by saying that at long last we were all together this time.'

Bill held the phone and didn't know what to say to Sheila. When it came to naming the date, he quite properly sat on his hands. The other delegates were in the same position. The NUPE conference decision for an all-out strike was now just a demand on the TUC.

The COHSE conference followed two weeks later. Albert Spanswick, the general secretary, spoke passionately against an all-out strike. Some at the conference agreed with him. Some just felt their members weren't ready for an all-out strike yet. The strike motion failed. But the union conference gave the leadership no authority to settle. So what to do next?

Incredibly, a three-day strike. The arithmetic was as before. Three times nothing is nothing. Three times £10 lost is £30 lost. A lot of places came out for all three days. Some picked two. Some picked one. The feeling was beginning to drain on many picket lines. On the other hand, quite a lot of hospitals which had so far done nothing were galvanised into action. They were enthusiastic.

The real killer in the three-day strike was what it did to the prospects of building outside support. We were madly running around the docks, the print, the mines, the steel and the shipyards. They were big workplaces with strong traditions. People would sit up if they came out.

It wasn't easy to walk into the docks or the mines and ask for support for a three-day strike. They looked at you with the friendly pity of wise old men. What was the point, they asked, of a three-day strike? What were we playing at? They couldn't argue for their blokes to come out for three days. It was lunatic. Their lads knew it was all or nothing. But tell you what, we'll try for a one-day stoppage. Have you got a demonstration we could take the lads to? No? Well, get one fast.

It was harder to organise the three-day strike than anything we'd organised before. But the 'quality' press suddenly made Health Minister Norman Fowler into a scapegoat. They said he was being unreasonable and should concede. He started calling the TUC in for talks. He conceded another 0.5 per cent almost every day. In the end, we had an extra 1.5 per cent for the nurses and 2 per cent for the ancillaries. It wasn't enough. But the stewards could point to the members: the strikes do work, we're moving them.

The government wasn't moving just because the hospital workers were striking. It looked like the railways were coming out for themselves. The NUR executive had instructed its members to come out over the national pay offer on the railways. They had also instructed their members on the London Underground to come out, and there was talk of the buses coming out too. The capital would be crippled. Everybody notices a transport strike. If it was going on at the same time as a hospital strike, there would be movement in the air. People would start to feel their power. Other workers might come out, too. The government tried to buy off the hospital workers. They didn't try hard enough. The union negotiators rejected the offer.

The rail strike promptly collapsed. The executive had called a strike without balloting the membership. They didn't want to strike. The NUR conference called the strike off on its first day.

Two days later, the government told the train drivers' union (ASLEF) that they would have to give up their eight-hour day for 'flexible rostering'. They were forced out on strike. Management threatened to sack all of them unless they gave in. The TUC withdrew their support and told ASLEF to throw in the towel. ASLEF threw it in. The settlement negotiated by the TUC was a total defeat.

The effect on hospital workers was unfortunate. The government could now sit back and deal with them at its leisure. The militants in the hospitals had been arguing that the only way to win was an all-out strike. Like the railways, we said, and everybody cheered. That looked a bit sick now.

The most demoralising effect was what it showed about the TUC. They simply didn't have the bottle to stand up to the government. Many in the labour movement told themselves that the railway dispute was very complicated and there were all sorts of rivalries between ASLEF and the NUR. In the hospitals, nobody was quite that unrealistic. We were marching into battle behind the TUC. We were inclined to take a very careful look indeed at our generals. We didn't like what we saw.

We waited for what the TUC would do next. We'd had a one-day strike, a two-day strike and a three-day strike. Some jokers said that nothing could be more natural than a four-day strike. Nobody quite believed the TUC would be that thick. The TUC opted for a five-day strike.

Some places did indeed come out for all five days. Most places, the stewards and the members couldn't face it. They wanted to know what good a five-day strike would be. The TUC said it would help to reduce the NHS to working on an accident and emergency basis. The stewards and the members usually decided to try to achieve that with sectional strikes.

These had been a success in many areas already. Some hospitals had had sections out for twelve weeks. In most general hospitals quite small sections can bring everything to a grinding halt. Stores, the laundry, the central sterile supplies department and the operating theatre are all crucial. The union collected a levy from all the members in the hospital. This made up the lost wages of the dozen or twenty strikers. Management usually had to agree to reduce the hospital to an accident and emergency basis. In return, the unions agreed to provide emergency cover in the striking section to service those beds.

The stewards recommended sectional strikes because they wanted to keep something going. They also wanted to bring local management to heel – just this once. The members voted for sectional strikes so they didn't have to lose five days' money. Things were definitely winding down.

And there were problems with sectional strikes. Some sections did stay out for ten or twelve weeks. But they all eventually came to an end. For one thing, people got tired of being on picket duty all day. Collecting the levy got harder and harder. The reason it got harder was that nobody could see what good it was doing. It reduced the number of patients. Fine. That didn't seem to bother anybody apart from those on the waiting list. Management was moving to close the empty wards and lay people off.

The sectional strikes tended to isolate hospital workers. After all, you can't go and ask other people to strike in your support if you're not on strike yourself. Unlike a real strike, you just don't have a horde of people to go on flying pickets and talk to other workers. It's also a lot of work keeping a sectional strike together and raising a levy and running a picket line. It demands almost as much from the stewards as a real strike.

Sectional strikes also encourage the idea that union action is somebody else's business. You pay your dues and the men in the laundry or the miners strike for you. You're only a nurse. Nurses can't be expected to act for themselves, can they? They wouldn't know how, would they? Anyway, think of the patients.

The same thing was wrong with the sectional picket lines. Usually, the section and a few stewards would be on picket duty in front of the hospital. Every morning most of the union members would happily stream past the pickets into work. They weren't on strike, after all. Then the pickets would ask the lorries and the post van and the lift guards not to cross. By and large, they would turn away.

What was happening showed how little most hospital workers understood about what picket lines *mean*. Most workers won't cross one as long as they have a union of their own to fall back on. This isn't out of some generalised feeling of solidarity. It's because the people on that picket line are losing money day by day. They're not eating right, their families are hurting, the electricity board is threatening to cut them off. They're fighting for their working lives, and you respect them for it. Crossing that picket line is scabbing. But in the hospitals everybody was crossing. Other workers were being asked to respect the line by people who, in many cases, weren't really hurting.

And, of course, the sectional strikes did nothing to win the dispute. Most stewards running sectional strikes were only too well aware of that. They were just trying to keep something going inside the hospital while they figured out how to move the TUC.

The basic problem was this. Nothing less than an all-out strike was going to win. The TUC was running things. The TUC wasn't going to call an all-out strike. They were just going to keep calling token strikes till you were exhausted.

Nobody had an alternative to the TUC. There was no rank-and-file network in the hospitals that could move independently of the TUC. Remember that most cities and districts didn't have a joint shop stewards' committee. Many of the ones that did exist were largely talking shops. After four months of the dispute, many cities still only had strike committees of activists, not real stewards' committees. On a national level, there was nothing with enough standing to challenge the TUC control.

On a local level, there had been valiant efforts to start an all-out strike. In the wake of the NUPE conference decision there had been all-out strikes in Rotherham and in two Edinburgh hospitals. But in both cases the movements had been too small. The workers couldn't spread the action to other hospitals or other industries. They went back to work.

So the hospital workers waited to see that the TUC would do. Demoralisation crept up as the weeks wore on. The stewards and activists were done in. Many of them had gone sick: their bodies were telling them to slow down. Then a funny thing happened. The TUC conference in September was all about militant support for the hospital workers.

The General Council had considerable problems going into the conference. They had a lot of explaining to do. They had to sell the delegates their support for the Labour right and the attack on Militant. They also had to justify their own craven behaviour in the train drivers' dispute. Not easy. What they did, in effect, was to change the subject. Speaker after speaker advanced to the rostrum. Each delivered ringing words about how the whole labour movement must pull together against Thatcher by supporting the hospital workers. The emphasis on duty and fighting the Tories disposed of those who might quibble about what was happening in the Labour Party. In the conference corridors there were whispers about ASLEF. There had been all that rivalry between Ray Buckton and Sid Weighell, and the whole thing had been very complicated. Best not to rake up that old stuff, really. Because now the hospital workers need all our support and we really mean it this time . . .

Exactly what our leaders really meant was not 100 per cent clear. It was clear enough they didn't mean an all-out strike in the hospitals, with support from other unions. Possibly Bickerstaffe of NUPE and Spanswick of COHSE still thought that something less stood a chance. It's not possible that David Basnett, of the GMBATU, or Moss Evans, of the TGWU, thought that one-day strikes would win. They were both men with too much experience within the strong sections of the labour movement. Nor is it likely that Arthur Scargill thought the one-day strikes would win.

The TUC wanted to win the dispute. But not if it meant really taking on the government. That much was clear. Little else was. There was a one-day strike already fixed for 22 September. The obvious move was to support this. Despite the speeches, few union executives actually instructed their members to strike on that day. Instead, they recommended, or encouraged, them to participate in a day of action – whatever that meant.

In truth, the union leaders weren't at all sure their members would follow a strike call. They often didn't take their own rhetoric seriously. But one group of people did take them at their word.

The TUC conference is shown on television every afternoon. Highlights are shown in the evening. Among the few people who watch it are the leading activists on the shop floor. They themselves treasure a secret ambition to be a TUC delegate one year. They take its proceedings seriously. Though they have considerable reservations, they do tend to believe what their leaders say. They saw their general secretary call for support for the hospital workers. They decided it was their duty to start organising that support.

There had certainly been support from other workers already. But most of the organising had been done by hospital workers and revolutionaries. It was they who went around visiting workplaces, got hospital workers invited to speak, and so on. Now, stewards from all over were deluging the hospitals with phone calls asking for speakers. They were arguing endlessly with their members in bus garages and offices.

The hospital workers caught the imagination of the working class. There were several reasons for this. First, they were the angels of mercy. Every time a steward asked for a speaker, he said please could at least one speaker be a nurse. He was a little embarrassed about it. He explained that he knew all hospital workers were in it together. But his members went on about the nurses. They were a little backward, really, and didn't realise it was a class thing. But could they have a nurse?

The propaganda had backfired. If the angels of mercy were that badly paid, then other workers had to help them. They couldn't win on their own without endangering patients' lives. There was something here of chivalry. Nobody actually said anything, but we were terribly tempted to send pretty young nurses to do the speaking. The *Yorkshire Miner* replaced its nude pin-up of the month with a picture of a fully clothed nurse on the picket line. There was also something of gratitude. It turned out that the ads were right. People do remember nurses.

There was something more going on as well: a stirring of class feeling. You could see it when you spoke at mass meetings. The meeting would begin with a speech by a couple of hospital workers about why we wanted support. Then the stewards and convenor would come in with why they should strike. 'It isn't just them,' they said, 'Look what's happening to us.' The stewards on the bins talked about privatisation. The dockers talked about redundancies. On the post, they talked about second deliveries and changes in rosters and shifts. In each case, they were talking about looming attacks. In each case, the workers didn't see how they could fight back.

One building site was typical. Ken Livingstone's GLC was wrapping up its direct labour force and replacing those workers with contractors. The work on that particular site was coming to an end. The lads were all taking their redundancy. For middle-aged men in a collapsing construction industry, that was a one-way ticket to misery and the dole. The convenor tried to interest the lads in a one-day strike against the GLC. Why bother, said the lads. You can't win. Yet at the same time, the lads started pushing the convenor to get a nurse down to speak. They were fully prepared to come out for the nurses.

It was the same in a lot of places. It surprised the stewards all right. Suddenly, people who were stuck in apathy and wouldn't fight for themselves were fighting for the hospitals. It seemed contradictory.

The reason they wouldn't fight for themselves was the same reason they would fight for the hospital workers. The slump. For eight years the Callaghan and Thatcher governments had pushed through cuts and redundancies. Most strikes had ended in defeat. There were four million unemployed and more to come. People were overwhelmed. They were being attacked as a class, and yet they were being picked off one by one. It would take a massive fight to beat the government. They couldn't see it happening. They felt hopeless and took the redundancy money. They then felt depressed and helplessly angry.

Along came the hospital workers. This was a national strike, called by the TUC. The isolation was over. It was a change to show how you felt. 'We may not be able to do anything about the mess in this office, but by God we can come out for the hospital workers.'

There were other reasons they came out too. The stewards and convenors at the mass meetings went on about the threat to the NHS and all the hospitals that had closed. The cuts campaigns had seemed almost a waste of time. All that knocking on doors and going on to stewards about the closures and giving them badges and petitions to sign. They hadn't been able to do anything then. But they had remembered. And now they were telling their members about it.

Perhaps the most important reason people came out was that the hospital workers actually had the confidence to ask them. Most workers on strike feel isolated and defensive. We stood up and told them that we were providing emergency cover because it was their mums and dads in that hospital. They'd *have* to strike to support us. We spent our working lives caring for people, with few thanks and little money. We felt the working class owed it to us to support us in our need.

That gave us the confidence to go back and back. At my hospital, we went down to the town hall every time we came out. The first time, we gave the NALGO steward some leaflets. The second time, we talked to three NALGO stewards. The third time, two of them stood with us in their lunch hour. The fourth time, they arranged a mass meeting for us to speak to. The fifth time, ten of them stood on our picket line. The sixth time, they had their own picket line and struck in our support. Their picket line was better than ours.

That was the one-day strike on 22 September. Nationally, it was patchy. Support from the public services was far stronger than from private industry. Spanswick went on television to beg the rail workers not to join in. He said trains were needed to take people to demonstrations. The railways didn't strike. The unions mostly did no more than 'advise' their members to take 'appropriate' action. But the strike showed the power that was there. It was the largest solidarity strike since 1926. A watershed in class consciousness had been crossed. If the TUC pulled itself together, the strength was there to smash the government. Hospital militants had been on the point of despair. On the day, the demonstrations were magnificent. People who had given up allowed themselves to hope. They told themselves the TUC couldn't sabotage this sort of feeling.

They could. In fact they reached new imaginative heights. First, they called a series of one-day regional strikes. The one-day national strike hadn't moved the government. What would a regional strike do? The strikes happened here one week and there another week. The feeling of shared power was fragmented. A few workplaces did come out in solidarity. Most hospitals hung on grimly. But the writing was on the wall.

Next the TUC called a one-day strike by hospital workers and transport workers. Other workers were told not to strike. And the union leaders had just sold the transport workers down various rivers. The TGWU baggage handlers at Heathrow had gone down to an isolated defeat. The engine drivers had been deserted, the NUR thrashed. London Transport had accepted fare rises and staffing cuts. The dockers had been ready to fight to extend their job-guarantee scheme to the unregistered ports. The TGWU called off the action to keep the blood flowing in the Falklands. Now the TUC had come back to ask these same workers for support. At the same time, they were holding back on any other activity.

The hospital workers reluctantly agreed to come out again. By now, it was hard to find anybody who thought anything less than an all-out strike would win. But they just couldn't bring themselves to cave in. The stewards emphasised it was an official call. There are all these other people striking for us. The least we can do is strike with them. Cuts and privatisation are coming. Any hospital that stays in will be marked down as a soft option.

Our hospital voted to strike. But there were murmurs that some would scab. There was considerable resentment among the ancillaries about the nurses. The press had gone on about the nurses this, the nurses that. The cleaners knew that they had stayed solid for months. Most of the nurses had crossed the picket line time after time. The cleaners felt used.

The heart had gone out of the picket line. In May, twenty enthusiastic nurses had hurrahed on the picket line. In the regional one-day strike in October, two stewards stood on the line alone until ten in the morning.

The transport strike was due to start on Monday. After the last mass meetings were over, the TUC panicked – on Friday night. Reports from the docks and the stations said many areas weren't coming out. The TUC were afraid their weakness would be exposed. They called off the strike, and exposed their weakness themselves.

That was that. The pay campaign was effectively over. The TUC had little option but to accept the offer. They had to refer it to the members, though.

They said, 'Look, there are two choices. Either we have an all-out strike or we accept what's on offer. No other tactics will change the government.'

Most people had known this for months. There is a tide in the affairs of men which, taken at the flood, leads on to victory. So it is said, and we have no reason to doubt it. The TUC were taking it at the ebb, and leading on to defeat. For months they had called one useless one-day strike after another. Not once had they turned round and explained that their tactics weren't going to win it. Not once had the NUPE leadership taken the argument for an all-out strike to the membership. Now, when their members were exhausted and demoralised, they were suddenly going on about all-out strike. It let them off the hook. Look, we didn't sell out. The members just wouldn't fight. Now we saw the true beauty of the one-day strike as a tactic.

My NUPE branch was typical. We had a mass meeting. Thirty-three people came, which was average for our small hospital. Twenty-seven voted to accept the offer. Six voted for an all-out strike. There wasn't much dissension in the meeting. The six didn't really expect an all-out strike. We were registering a protest. The twenty-seven were more bitter towards the TUC than the six. One of the twenty-seven put it well. 'If we'd all come out in June we would have won. The TUC doesn't care, with their mortgages and their cars – they're all right. I tell you straight, I'm voting to accept. I don't think there's any point any longer. But at least we've learned something. That's about all you can say for this year. We've learned something.'

5. Pray!

The 1982 pay campaign ended in defeat. In the last chapter I was a bit hard on the TUC. Really, their weakness was no surprise. That had always been there. The surprise was that they led their first national strike since 1926. (They sold that one out in nine days flat, but there was more urgency then.)

Why did they lead it? On the one hand, the hospital workers themselves and their individual unions didn't feel strong enough to fight alone. They needed the national unity of all hospital workers. Since the rank and file had no organisation of their own, they had to go through the TUC. That meant failure.

On the other hand, the hospital workers did feel bitter enough to fight. It was our bitterness that kept us going all those months. At the beginning, every experienced militant in the hospitals assumed we would come out for three one-day strikes at most. Then it would be over. We were wrong. The hospital workers hung on grimly. They complained in mass meetings, they threatened to scab, they moaned about the union leaders. But they hung on.

In the end, it wasn't the TUC that mattered. It was the workers. Remember the NUPE conference. The delegates there wanted an all-out strike. But they knew the members as a whole hadn't been persuaded. So they hung back. The COHSE conference, too, had no mandate from the members for an all-out strike.

Perhaps better leadership would have changed this. Perhaps not. The NUR executive and the NUM executive both wanted a strike in 1982 and couldn't carry their members. The real trouble was a contradiction in the heads of the hospital workers. They share it with the rest of the working class. It was seen in the battle against the cuts, it was seen in the pay campaign, and it will be seen again. It goes like this.

The working class is living through massive change. The system is in crisis and will stay in crisis. Unemployment will go up. Real wages will go down. Public services are falling apart. Things are going to get worse. From now on, we only get what we fight for. We are fighting a ruthless and intelligent enemy. The ruling class has little room to manoeuvre. They have to break us. We have to fight back . . .

That's reality. It's unpleasant. Better not to think about it. There must be some way for reasonable people to work things out. They can't really mean to close this children's hospital, this steelworks, this shipyard. It must be they don't understand what that would mean.

That's one way to avoid what's happening. Another way is to hope it happens to somebody else. The convenor walks down to the shop floor and announces management want a hundred redundancies. A voice asks, 'Which section?' On a larger level, the workers in a hospital argue they should be left alone because they're treating women or children or cancer. On a global level, British steel workers petition their government to impose import controls so that steel workers in Poland and America will lose their jobs.

What's happening is that people still have in their heads the ideas which served them so well for so long. Now the world has changed. But its inhabitants are still stuck with the old ideas and the old leaders.

Now the hospital workers brace themselves for what comes next. Almost immediately after the strike the government announced plans to 'privatise' the hospital laundries, cleaning and catering. This would mean putting out the work to private contractors. This is supposed to be more efficient. It is unlikely to provide a cheaper or a better service, though it will lead to redundancies and demoralisation among workers. It will also make a tidy little profit for the contractors. At times, the Thatcher government seems to represent not the class interests of the capitalists but the collective consciousness of the demolition sub-contractors.

For two years my job involved doing occasional work on the children's ward in a small hospital run by fundamentalist Christians. I went up to the ward once. The children were crippled by spinal diseases. Devoted nurses fed them by hand. I told my boss I would do anything I was asked for that ward, but I couldn't bear to go back there again.

In December 1982, management announced they were closing that hospital within the month. The children would be transferred to another hospital, itself slated for closure in two years. The adult beds would be lost. The unions felt helpless. We had just lost a national strike and a local victimisation case. We were too weak to fight that month. Management knew it. They no longer felt they had to observe even the elementary proprieties. They felt free to close the children's ward in a Christian hospital over Christmas. The staff there issued a leaflet calling for protest. The main tactic advocated in the leaflet was simple: PRAY.

Sometimes it seems that we've tried everything else. Perhaps prayer is all that's left.

But really we could have won. The 1982 dispute showed that the feeling was there. Both among hospital workers and in the working class as a whole. It also showed that workers would strike for each other. If you sent out workers on strike to talk to each other and you kept sending them out, the class did move.

The feeling was there. The solidarity was there. What was missing was the understanding that we had to take on the government head on. We are being attacked as a class. It's a serious attack. We have to fight back as a class, in a serious manner. If we don't, we'd better pray our children don't get sick.

Colin Thunhurst

It Makes You Sick
The Politics of the NHS

How modern capitalism creates ill-health and profits from it/Why the progressive potential of the NHS has been undermined by successive governments/What sort of health service we should demand/How we can fight to get it

'Written with force, lucidity and precision' *New Statesman*

0-86104-503-3

David Hall

The Cuts Machine
The Politics of Public Expenditure

What the Tories plan to do to your health, homes and education/How they fix the figures to make it easier/Why the TUC and the Labour Party should come up with something better than the Alternative Economic Strategy/Why we must fight for jobs, services and democratic controls

'In this short but extremely lucid book... David Hall puts it all in political perspective... offers a clear account of the mechanics of public expenditure' *Guardian*

0-86104-504-1

Lesley Doyal with Imogen Pennell

The Political Economy of Health

Shows how ill-health reflects the social and economic organisation of society/The value to capital of a healthy workforce/How health services control and socialise people/Why medicine is big business

'Readable and well researched... a stimulating book and a worthy contribution to current debates on the politics of health' *Lancet*

'Mandatory reading' *New Statesman*

'The turning point in the study of health, illness and health care' *Marxism Today*

0-86104-074-0 paperback
0-86104-075-9 hardback